CROSSCURRENTS *Modern Critiques*

CROSSCURRENTS *Modern Critiques*
Harry T. Moore, *General Editor*

Richard Rees

George Orwell FUGITIVE
FROM THE CAMP OF VICTORY

WITH A PREFACE BY

Harry T. Moore

Carbondale

SOUTHERN ILLINOIS UNIVERSITY PRESS

FIRST PUBLISHED, FEBRUARY 1962
SECOND PRINTING, SEPTEMBER 1962
ARCTURUS BOOKS Ⓡ EDITION, MARCH 1965

IT IS APPROPRIATE that the volume on George Orwell in the Crosscurrents series has been written by Sir Richard Rees, not just because he was among the first to publish and encourage Orwell, but also because he writes of the man and his work with valuable insight and enviable skill.

Orwell is particularly noted for his criticism of the world we live in; but it is a criticism which, even in its satirical extremes, is not tinged with personal bitterness. In this he differs from Swift, whom he in some ways resembles, and about whom he wrote a brilliant essay. Like Swift, Orwell was a master of plain prose that had nothing in it of the ornamental or the finicky. His writing went in a clean, hard line.

This quality of Orwell's was apparent in one of the early sketches Richard Rees mentions prominently in the present book: "The Spike," which as part of Orwell's book, Down and Out in Paris and London, retains its force. Rees published "The Spike" in the Adelphi under Orwell's own name, Eric Blair. I can remember asking Rees at the time who this new author was who wrote so powerfully, and he told me a little about him. Rees later became better acquainted with Orwell, and in this volume he gives us his seasoned memories of the man. These come at the end;

before that, he provides us with a penetrating study of Orwell's work.

In previous books, Sir Richard Rees has made an illuminating comparison of D. H. Lawrence and Simone Weil (Brave Men), an instructive collection of the critical writings of his friend the late John Middleton Murry, and (in For Love or Money) a cogent examination of modern values. In the present volume he shows above all why Orwell is an important writer and why, across these years when so many literary idols have been left to gather dust in neglected temples, he has survived to be read and studied.

HARRY T. MOORE

January 1961

CONTENTS

George Orwell

FUGITIVE FROM THE CAMP OF VICTORY

1 JUSTICE

> Si on sait par où la société est déséquilibrée, il faut faire
> ce qu'on peut pour ajouter du poids dans le plateau trop
> léger. . . . Mais il faut avoir conçu l'équilibre, et être
> toujours prêt à changer de côté, comme la Justice, cette
> "fugitive du camp des vainqueurs."
>
> Simone Weil, *Cahiers*, III, 84

THIS BOOK IS ABOUT George Orwell's books . . . If
you have not already closed it after reading that sentence, it is because you are a child of our age. We
have books about books, plays about the theatre, and
movies about Hollywood. (As long ago as 1935 George
Orwell gloomily described the cinema as the art that
was destined to replace literature. We have not yet
reached that point, however, and in the meantime
we have literature about literature and criticism of
criticism ad infinitum.) If there is any justification for
the present study of Orwell it is that he is famous
mainly on account of two books—*Animal Farm* and
1984—while the rest of his work is comparatively little
known. A study which tries to show the whole of his
work in perspective may succeed in bringing out the
importance of some of the earlier books, and this may
possibly throw some new light on the two most famous ones. This book, therefore, is intended as an
introduction to Orwell. To the books rather than to
the man, in so far as the two can be separated; but, as

will appear very clearly in these pages, a proper appreciation of the books depends upon knowing something both about the man and about the period in which he lived.

IN HIS ESSAY "Politics vs. Literature" Orwell says of Swift that "politically he was one of those people who are driven into a sort of perverse Toryism by the follies of the progressive party of the moment," and Orwell himself has sometimes been described in much the same way by hostile critics. It is true that he criticized the follies of "the progressive party of the moment" and his criticisms were indeed Swiftian. But he never ceased to criticize reactionaries also, and his attacks owed their sting to the fact that he was a more genuine progressive than his Communist opponents and a better conservative than his reactionary opponents. He was against bullying, whoever it was that was being bullied. He was, in fact, a just man in Simone Weil's sense of the word justice.

In any social order force is necessarily inherent, and force is always liable to turn into bullying. Force is only negated when there is a true balance. As Simone Weil said,

> If one knows in what respect society is unbalanced, one must do what one can to add weight to the lighter of the two scales. Although the weight is bound to be evil, by using it with the intention of re-establishing the balance it may be that one avoids any personal degradation. But one must first of all have clearly recognised where the balance lies, and be always ready to change sides, like Justice, that "fugitive from the victors' camp."

It would be difficult to imagine a better statement of the principles upon which Orwell seems always instinctively to have acted.

One of the most obvious examples of disequilibrium in society is that the interests of the rich outweigh the interests of the poor, and here Orwell's weight was always added to the lighter side; but his sense of balance was exceptionally acute and when the scales were tampered with he would always be among the first to feel it and the most courageous in protesting. He was one of those writers, like Joseph Conrad, Simone Weil, and Arthur Koestler, whose life and work are interconnected in such a way that it is difficult to think of the work without also thinking of the life, and vice versa. But he was a "born writer" and in a happier age—or at least a calmer and more stable one, for how can we judge the happiness of an age? —one can imagine him devoting himself to prose fiction as single-mindedly as Flaubert or Jane Austen.

In the circumstances of his time, however, he was driven into political polemic, and his two most famous books, although they are classifiable as fiction, are in fact politico-social fables. Indeed, apart from his first four books, nearly everything he wrote had a political slant. Even his essays on Dickens and Kipling, though they are admirable literary criticism, are something else as well. And two of his best books, *Down and Out in Paris and London* and *Homage to Catalonia*, are autobiographical narratives—the first slightly rearranged and the second as straightforward as a diary— of which the former has a sociological and the latter a political interest apart from their artistic value. As a pure novelist his achievement was less outstanding though his promise was considerable, and his fourth novel, *Coming up for Air*, suggests that he had potentialities which could have been developed much further. But in any case between 1934 and 1939 he wrote four novels which are certainly better worth rereading today than most of the serious fiction produced in those years.

ORWELL'S TEMPERAMENT and character, like most people's, were complex. It is easy to distinguish at least four separate and sharply contrasting strains in him. First, there is the rebel Orwell, whose rebelliousness was profound and comprehensive. It began, Prometheus-like, with defying Zeus himself. Life is unjust and tragic; the innocent suffer and the righteous are oppressed; and Orwell could neither blind himself to these facts nor be reconciled to them. The rebel Orwell was a profoundly serious and tragic pessimist; but his pessimism did not entail resignation nor prevent him from fighting injustice in every field in which he met it.

The second Orwell, who at first sight contrasts surprisingly with the rebellious champion of minorities, is sympathetic to authority, at least so long as it is benign and paternal. He feels respect for men in responsible positions and is a scathing and scourging critic of irresponsible critics. This is the Orwell who admires Joseph Conrad and, with reservations, defends Kipling. Thirdly, there is the rationalist Orwell, the tenacious heir of the eighteenth-century *Éclaircissement*. Like the authoritarian Orwell, he is a powerful debunker of spurious idealism and spirituality. It is his eighteenth-century phlegm and enlightened rationality that inspire Orwell's swift and plain and serviceable prose style. The fourth Orwell is a romantic, a lover of the past, of quaint Dickensian streets and homes, of quiet fishing streams and of old-fashioned virtues, old-fashioned customs and old-fashioned people. These four heterogeneous strains were combined in him to form a well-balanced and harmonious character which might have been a happy one, in spite of his philo-

sophic pessimism, if the times in which he lived had
been less unpropitious.

But this diagrammatic fourfold Orwell is of course
a grotesque oversimplification. It does not even show
his two most conspicuous and arresting characteristics,
though there is no difficulty in relating them to the
diagram. One of these characteristics is a school-boy-
ish love of adventure and action and the other is a hy-
persensitive conscience, almost amounting to a guilt
complex, which drove him to extremes of expiatory
self-abasement for crimes not his own. No one who
reads his account in *Homage to Catalonia* of his life
as a militia corporal on the Aragon front or of the street
fighting in Barcelona can doubt that he, in some sense,
enjoyed this kind of thing; * but I believe his readiness
to expose himself to it was also connected with his respect for men burdened with practical responsibilities
and with his contempt for sentimental uplift and arm-
chair idealism. And it is easy to connect his sense of
guilt with his unrelenting awareness of the injustices
and degradations which men suffer as the result of
other men's selfishness and callousness.

But everything human is ambivalent. The urge to
expiate human suffering by exposing oneself to degradation is connected with a defiant Promethean arrogance which Orwell himself describes in the semi-au-
tobiographical hero of *Keep the Aspidistra Flying* as
"an evil mutinous mood." In general, it seems often
to be true that the most heroic and even saintly virtues
are mysteriously related to a kind of egoism which may
not be greater but is more active and virulent than that
of ordinary men. There *is* a sense in which the Orwell

* And this although he was so kindhearted that when he saw a
Fascist soldier running along a trench and simultaneously trying to
pull up his trousers, he was unable to bring himself to fire—a man
trying to pull up his trousers is a fellow human being and not a
Fascist, he argued.

who nearly starved in Paris and who tramped from workhouse to workhouse in London was giving way to a mood of sulky rebellion against life. He was also, however, exhibiting a kind of integrity and steadfastness almost unique in his generation.

HAVING HAD the advantage of knowing him well during the last twenty of his forty-seven years of life, I am able to draw from time to time upon my personal knowledge of him, and I have also included a final chapter, collecting what seem to me the more significant of my scattered memories of him over twenty years. It may seem superfluous to begin by saying that he was an extremely intelligent man. But he was not by nature competitive and anything in the way of exhibitionism or "showing off" was entirely alien to his character. For this reason it was easy to underestimate the acuteness and power of his mind; and his readers are equally likely to be misled by his unpretentious and straightforwardly simple style. His chief limitation, perhaps, was his lack of interest in philosophy and psychology. The interest in new psychological theories was at its height during his early days as a writer, but I have no recollection of his ever once mentioning the name of Freud or Jung, or Kafka, or even Dostoevsky. This psychological incuriosity was a limitation, but I am not sure that it was altogether detrimental to his writing. As regards philosophy, he was typically English in possessing a naturally positivist outlook; and it was perhaps his mature eighteenth-century common sense, rather than philosophical incuriosity, that made him indifferent to linguistic and logical analysis, for which, if he had been sufficiently interested, he probably had a gift. He was equally unimpressed by the existentialist philosophies in vogue toward the end of his life and here, I think, there was a temperamental

barrier; though it might nevertheless be claimed that
he was in real life a better existentialist, more authen-
tic and more "engaged," than many philosophers
whose existentialism exists mainly between the covers
of a book.

His passion for literature was lifelong and dated from
very early years; and if we consider only his first three
deeply pessimistic novels he appears in some ways to
resemble George Gissing. He has the same resolute,
plodding honesty, and although his novels are not
showy, there is more meat in them than in their brilliant ephemeral competitors. But whereas Gissing appeared to be working, from economic necessity, in an
antipathetic medium and to be at bottom a thwarted
essayist and classicist, Orwell seemed perfectly at
home both in the novel and in his later political writing. Both Gissing and Orwell, however, shared the
melancholy of men who see the world moving in a direction uncongenial to them.

It is often, perhaps always, a function of the serious
and responsible intellectual to go against the prevail-
ing current of his times. It is merely another aspect of
Simone Weil's conception of Justice as the seeker of
balance. But it is hard work and it takes a heavy toll.
When one considers how many of the finest intellectuals, in this century alone, have died early from consumption—Chekhov, Katherine Mansfield, D. H.
Lawrence, Simone Weil, and Orwell, for example—it
seems reasonable to ask whether this disease may not
sometimes be connected with the strain and effort of
swimming against the stream.

DID ORWELL, in some sense, die of despair? Probably
the most succinct and penetrating appreciation ever
written of him is the one by Bertrand Russell in *World
Review* (June, 1950), and it might seem to justify this

conclusion. Orwell had wide interests, Russell points out, and "would have been genial if he had lived at a less painful time"; he was even capable of considering sympathetically Dickens' belief that all would be well if people would behave well and that it is not the reform of institutions that is really important. But unlike the majority of so-called realists and so-called idealists Orwell was capable of facing reality. As he wrote in a criticism of H. G. Wells: "What is the use of pointing out that a World State is desirable? All sensible men for decades past have been substantially in agreement with what Mr. Wells says, but sensible men have no power. Hitler is a criminal lunatic, and he has an army of millions of men." Unlike the liberal rationalist, Orwell faced the fact that "sensible men have no power." According to Russell this caused him to lose hope. He certainly lost—what in spite of the eighteenth-century cast of his mind he had never completely held—the illusions of the rationalist optimist who thinks that reason, in his own limited understanding of the word, is or ever could be all-powerful in human affairs. And indeed the reader of 1984 may easily conclude that its author must have died in utter despair. There was a time, however, when he was groping towards a soberer, less Utopian, and more solidly based optimism; though it is true that this also seems to have evaporated almost, though perhaps not quite, completely by the time he wrote 1984. How he acquired this glimpse of a more profoundly reasonable optimism, and why it faded, will be one of the inquiries raised in this book.

HIS WRITINGS will be discussed in chronological order, but with anticipatory references in the earlier chapters to his later and better known work. Since all his books, including the novels, up to 1939 are to some extent

autobiographical, it may be useful before discuss
them to outline briefly the facts of his life.

Orwell's real name was Eric Arthur Blair. He wa
born in Bengal where his father, Richard Walmesley
Blair, was a civil servant. His childhood was passed in
the south of England and he went to a preparatory
school on the south coast. This school was prepared to
take a boy at a reduced fee if he seemed likely to gain
credit for it by winning a scholarship to one of the
great Public Schools, and Orwell was taken on those
terms. In due course he won a scholarship to Eton in
1916. (The description of Eton as a "public" school is
misleading to anyone unfamiliar with English educa-
tional terminology. A Public School is in fact an
exclusive and expensive boarding school for boys aged
approximately thirteen to eighteen.) After leaving
Eton, Orwell served for five years in the Imperial
Police in Burma, but on returning to England on
leave in 1927 he resigned and decided to become a
writer. In 1928–29 he lived in Paris but had little success in selling his work and was finally reduced to taking jobs as a *plongeur*, or dishwasher, in hotels and
restaurants. He returned to England destitute and
lived for a time as a tramp, but eventually got a teach-
ing job in a school in the outer London suburbs, and
later as a bookseller's assistant in Hampstead. During
this period (1929–34) he produced two books under
his pseudonym of George Orwell. The first, *Down and
Out in Paris and London* (1933), was an account of
his experiences in 1928–29, and the second was a
novel, *Burmese Days* (1934). The setting of the latter
was derived of course from his experiences in the Imperial Police.

From 1934 onward he was able to earn a meager
living by his pen. In his second novel, *The Clergyman's Daughter* (1935), he drew upon his experience

as a tramp and as a school teacher. In 1936 he married and in the same year there appeared his third novel, *Keep the Aspidistra Flying*. In this year, too, he made a tour of Lancashire and Yorkshire to study the living conditions of the unemployed miners. His observations were published in *The Road to Wigan Pier* (1937). At the end of 1936 he went to Spain, theoretically as a free-lance reporter of the civil war. But on arrival in Barcelona he enlisted in a unit of the socialist militias. After nearly six months at the front he was wounded, and almost immediately afterward he was involved in the street fighting in Barcelona when the unit to which he was attached was denounced as "Trotskyist" and suppressed. Escaping from the political police he returned to England, where he wrote an account of these adventures (*Homage to Catalonia*, 1938).

At this time his never very robust health began to break down, and he was under observation for tuberculosis of the lungs. The tests proved negative, but he was advised to spend the winter abroad, which he did in Morocco, returning to England in the spring of 1939. In that year his fourth novel, *Coming up for Air*, was published. During the war he lived in London and worked for a time in a department of the B.B.C. responsible for broadcasts to India. His book of essays, *Inside the Whale*, appeared in 1940 and a long essay, *The Lion and the Unicorn*, in 1941. In 1945 his wife died, just after they had adopted a baby. In the same year he published *Animal Farm*.

From 1946 to 1949 he lived mainly on the island of Jura in the Inner Hebrides, and his health steadily deteriorated. Apart from a volume of critical essays (1946), published in America as *Dickens, Dali and Others*, and a long essay, *The English People* (1947), he published no more books until 1949, when *1984* appeared. In the same year he was obliged to leave Jura and go to a sanatorium in the south of England. He married for the second time, and moved to London, hoping to go on to a sanatorium in Switzerland. But he died in London in January, 1950.

Two volumes of essays were published posthumously: *Shooting an Elephant* (1950) and *England, Your England* (1953). The latter was published in America as *Such, Such Were the Joys*, the essay of that name not being included in the English edition. The contents of his four volumes of essays are listed in detail in the bibliographical note at the end of this book.

> *I think about evry bilding I pass an evry door in them got
> a iron flandge on it to keep they brothers out who want to
> rob them. Oh Man I think dont talk brother talk to me.*
> —Warren Miller, *The Cool World*

"WHERE DOES DADDY *get* it?" The speaker was an impoverished science student and he was addressing a
baby in a luxurious pram in the fashionable section of
Hyde Park, London. This angry young man, not having a rich Daddy and not being able to get hold of
enough money, felt himself condemned to stagnate in
the dreary and static lower-middle class, and excluded
from the progressive world of science and art. He was
a typical H. G. Wells hero of the early years of this
century.

A generation later, in 1936, George Orwell depicted,
in *Keep the Aspidistra Flying,* the frustration and fury
of a penniless young writer whose poverty and lack of
social influence prevented the acceptance of his poems
by the editors of high-class reviews. In the end he ca-
pitulated to the social system he despised, by marry-
ing respectably and getting a job in an advertising firm.

Some twenty years later still, in the nineteen-fifties,
Mr. John Osborne showed on the stage a hysterically
angry young man nagging at his wife about her superior middle-class habits, complaining that there was no
place in society for a man of his intellectual qualifica-

tions, and refusing to undertake any more ambitious work than running a sweetshop, or candy store.

It might seem that the angry young man is a perennial feature of the English literary scene. But there are interesting differences in his successive manifestations in Wells, Orwell and Osborne. By the time Osborne's young man appeared a good many of the genuine grievances of Wells's student had been abolished or mitigated. A considerable measure of social security, a vast extension of social services, many more opportunities of university education, and a drastic stepping-up of income tax had made England a noticeably less unequal society. Mr. Osborne's young man has fewer concrete grievances to complain about than his predecessors, which may account for the peevish, hysterical note in his anger. But at least there remains to him one mysterious and never-failing resource: the great intangible grievance of "class."

In spite of the fairly considerable steps toward equalization of incomes and opportunity that have been made in the twentieth century, England is still probably the most class-ridden society in the western world. But it would be more accurate to say class-*haunted*, for in actual fact the nineteenth-century social hierarchy has more or less collapsed. It is true of course that differences of status depend upon social power as well as upon money, but blue blood and heraldic quarterings are no longer of much avail in the struggle for social power—which is now almost as open and free for all as in the United States. Nevertheless the class bogey still stalks abroad, making hearts ache and scattering chips on shoulders. All this must be quite difficult for an American reader to understand, but unless he tries to do so he is in danger of missing the peculiar significance of Orwell in twentieth-century English letters.

At the time of Orwell's birth in 1903 almost everyone would have recognized, and not many would have criticized, the fact of the existence of three more or less clearly defined social classes: a small upper class of "gentlefolk," a big middle class, and a very big lower or "working" class. They shaded into one another of course, and with sufficient ingenuity it was possible to distinguish innumerable subdivisions. To be a member of the most exclusive, though not the most powerful or conspicuous, section of the upper class you had to belong to an "old" family—not necessarily a titled family but one which could trace its lineage and its high status back through many generations. Orwell once meticulously defined himself as a member of the "lower upper-middle class," and this was approximately correct. But the upper-middle class shaded into the upper class, and the qualification "lower" merely implied poorer, so he could equally well have described himself as an impoverished member of the upper class; and he possessed, in fact, many of the characteristics of a quite exclusive section of it. And at this point we encounter a further subtlety of the mysterious class-system: the fact that the word "gentleman," like the word "noble," was used in an ethical, not to say mystical, sense as well as in a technical social sense. "He's a *real* gentleman" was a genuine and heartfelt tribute often paid by members of the working class (less often of the middle class, because, in their case, class jealousy and susceptibility might enter in) to a member of the upper class of whose behavior they approved. It would have been hard to refuse the technical description of "gentleman" to any member of a very old family: but it was perfectly possible to say that he was not behaving like one. Conversely, you could praise the gentlemanliness of any member of any class, if you approved of his behavior; though if his speech and manners dif-

fered strikingly from upper-class standards you mi
qualify it: "one of *Nature's* gentlemen." This myst
conception of the gentleman as one who acts honor-
ably and behaves on all occasions with courtesy and
gentleness was a very confusing factor in the three-class
system, which might otherwise seem to be a fairly simple matter of grading society according to a combination of economic status and birth. It derives from a
myth, which itself derives from the Middle Ages, that
members of the nobility are by definition patterns of
gentlemanliness.

In Britain there still linger some strange and subtle
and deceptive echoes of the myth, and I believe its
power is obscurely present in the scene in Orwell's
Burmese Days where the hero, Flory, is humiliated on
the polo field by the aristocratic Verrall. This young
man, who dances and rides "with matchless grace"
and is almost monastically devoted to the cult of physical fitness, is detestably rude but is a gentleman in the
sense that he is a scion of a noble house. He does not,
however, behave like one; he behaves like a rude member of the upper class but not like a "real" gentleman.
And Flory, one feels, is not merely enraged but
shocked and *pained* by Verrall's rudeness. Although
Flory is clear sighted enough to see him without illusions as a young cub, he is nevertheless filled "with a
horrible sense of inferiority." It is true that Flory has
a sort of general inferiority complex, but it would not
normally enter into his reaction to a fellow country-
man's rudeness as it does in the incident with Verrall.

ORWELL'S FAMILY were not wealthy. His father was an
official in the Bengal Civil Service. But the family's
way of life was more upper-class than middle-class and
he himself, thanks to his ability to win scholarships,
obtained the most exclusive type of upper-class educa-

tion. From a fashionable preparatory school he passed at the age of thirteen into Eton, the most flamboyantly fashionable of all the so-called "Public" Schools.

Orwell, therefore, although he was brought up among boys of whom the majority, though by no means all, were richer than himself, had no logical reason for feeling any personal class grievance; and yet, as appears very clearly in the essay "Such, Such Were the Joys," where he describes his preparatory school, he had already acquired by the age of ten an outsize chip on his shoulder. If we could psychoanalyze him, should we find an explanation for it? Surely not, because psychoanalysis never gets beyond describing what happened; it can sometimes reveal, but it can never explain. Why, in a given set of circumstances, little Eric Arthur Blair turned into the writer George Orwell and died of consumption at the age of forty-seven, instead of becoming a juvenile delinquent, an aged valetudinarian, or a hundred other things, will always remain a mystery. But his extreme and morbid bitterness on finding himself among boys whose parents were in most cases paying higher fees than his own—an experience which was accepted by thousands of other boys—does seem to suggest a touch of perversity or "cussedness" in him from the start. We have already noted that Orwell himself acknowledged that the Promethean mood can have an evil mutinous aspect.

A pearl is the product of a diseased oyster; and men of remarkable gifts and character probably acquire them, in many cases, thanks to some obscure and unique irritation into which it is useless to inquire. In Orwell's case, however, it seems to me that there is one factor which would have made him a remarkable man, though not necessarily a writer, quite apart from any unique conditioning. I mean his passionately strong

sense of justice. It is arguable that this would be sufficient by itself to account for his bitterness at feeling
himself discriminated against, on account of his parents' poverty, by a snobbish schoolmaster. (But Mr.
Cyril Connolly at the same school and Mr. Christo-
pher Hollis at a similar one do not appear to have been
so sharply aware of this sort of discrimination, and it
seems very possible that Orwell's imagination exaggerated it.) But his attitude toward social and economic problems when he grew up was in any case almost certainly determined by the purest sense of
justice. He wrote, at the age of forty-five in his essay
"Why I Write," that we have developed "a sort of
compunction which our grandparents did not have, an
awareness of the enormous injustice and misery of the
world, and a guilt-stricken feeling that we ought to be
doing something about it." Maybe, but very few people feel this "sort of compunction" in the acute and
agonizing way he felt it. Both his life and his books
were deeply influenced, as we shall see, by his sense of
guilt for belonging to the upper class—indeed, for not
belonging to the lowest. It drove him to confess to the
world in *The Road to Wigan Pier* that he had grown
up believing that working class people smell worse
than others, and it was responsible for his tendency to
minimize the upper-class aspect of his own background.

Up to the age of about thirty he does not appear to
have seen politics as possessing any relevance to the
problem of justice as he conceived it. But when he did
make the connection he became, in the nineteen-
thirties, one of the very few left-wing intellectuals who
never lost sight of it. Being by temperament somewhat conservative, he was never seduced by any "wave
of the future." Socialism for him was a matter of conscience, not of taste or fashion or expediency, and in

his own very different terms he endorsed Blake's iden-
tification of politics and religion and brotherhood.
But his terms were so different from Blake's that he
eliminated religion altogether. In his eyes it was so
fouled by hypocrisy as to have become almost a dirty
word. As to brotherhood, his months with the anarchist and socialist militias in the Spanish civil war were
later to convince him that it might conceivably become a social reality, but he was under no illusion that
it actually existed anywhere in the circumstances of
contemporary social life, and it was not the sort of
word that came naturally to his pen.

"Dont talk brother talk to me" says the hero of *The
Cool World*, quoted at the head of this chapter. Mr.
Warren Miller's memorable novel about child gang-
sters in Harlem is in some ways a good example of
Orwellian realism—though it is doubtful if Orwell's
deus ex machina would have been a psychiatrist. But
nothing could be more Orwellian than the fourteen-
year-old gangster's reflections on brotherhood. How
much of it can there be in a city where anyone who
possesses anything worth stealing requires burglar-
proof locks to protect it? And of what city is this not
true? I've got mine, brother. You keep your hands off.

IT IS NECESSARY in any attempt to describe Orwell's
work to lay the first and heaviest stress upon his deep
and life-long preoccupation about the callousness of
"I'm all right, Jack; I've got mine." It was not so much
man's inhumanity to man but rather his self-absorption and sluggish indifference that was Orwell's permanent nightmare and torment. It stuck in his giz-
zard. He could not swallow it. And I doubt if he ever
succeeded in forgetting it for as much as twenty-four
hours in the whole of his adult life.

He was, naturally, sympathetic to beggars. "Why

are beggars despised?" he asks in *Down and Out in Paris and London:*

> I believe it is for the simple reason that they fail to earn a decent living. In practice nobody cares whether work is useful or useless, productive or parasitic; the sole thing demanded is that it shall be profitable. . . . A beggar, looked at realistically, is simply a business man, getting his living, like other business men, in the way that comes to hand. He has not, more than most modern people, sold his honour; he has merely made the mistake of choosing a trade at which it is impossible to grow rich.

Note that Orwell considers most modern people to have sold their honor. Beggars have merely sold theirs for a cheaper price. "Money," he says in the same passage, "has become the grand test of virtue. By this test beggars fail, and for this they are despised." The money test is an affront to human dignity and honor. Perhaps it was indifference to honor even more than indifference to justice that was Orwell's real preoccupation, and if he had been a hot-blooded Latin instead of a mild and rather austere Englishman who thought that good prose should be colorless "like a window pane," he might have written somewhat in the style of Bernanos.

It would be true, therefore, to call Orwell a deeply moral and earnest man. And yet it might be misleading. You can be deeply moral and earnest without being a good writer. You can be deeply moral and earnest and also a crashing bore. I would prefer to call him a conscience-stricken man. And although it was not his conscience that made him a writer, it was the sensitiveness, clarity and realism of his conscience that gave his writing its uniqueness and power. He was not particularly perspicacious in judging character, but he had a hawk's eye for detecting humbug in print or in an argument. In his own arguments he could be care-less about factual detail (in *Inside the Whale* he at-tributes to Auden a poem by Day Lewis and flagrantly misquotes Housman) and he sometimes made em-phatic statements based upon inadequate information. But on the deepest level he was an unwaveringly con-sistent and accurate thinker. Like an iron filing to a magnet his mind was oriented toward the simple truth that the world is full of injustice and that most of the attempts to reform it are hypocritical and half-hearted.

In his first book, *Down and Out in Paris and Lon-don*, he describes his own first-hand experience of the life of dishwashers in Paris hotels and tramps in Lon-don doss houses. One of the characters in the book who comes out well is a clergyman who is handing out meal tickets to a queue of tramps. Instead of adopting a hearty manner or improving the occasion by some words of uplift, he hurries along the line apologetically, with a shy and embarrassed look. Orwell notes that the men approved of this clergyman and expressed their approval by prophesying that *"He'll* never be a ———— bishop!" (It would not be surprising if some of them had added: "He's a *real* gentleman.") The point, of course, is that this clergyman did not kid him-self or them by trying to "talk brother talk." He felt and acknowledged the shamefulness of the whole sit-uation. Men without money, some of them subnormal and others skilled workers unable to find work, queu-ing up for official charity in the heart of London, a world centre of civilization.

And toward the end of his last book, 1984, Orwell makes his point with final, devastating clarity. The hero, who is in love with a girl called Julia, is the last individualist, the last champion of free thought and personal love, in a world of totalitarian bureaucracy founded upon brutality and lies. He is arrested and tortured, and what finally breaks his spirit is the loss of his self-respect; and he loses it after he has screamed out in his extremity:

> Do it to Julia! Do it to Julia! Not me! Julia! I don't care what you do to her. Tear her face off, strip her to the bones. Not me! Julia! Not me!

After this he knows how much he loves himself, and how much his love for Julia is worth. This knowledge breaks him, and he becomes a docile unit of the totalitarian state.

It is true that Orwell was in an advanced stage of consumption when he wrote this book; and it is possible, though sometimes difficult, to find gleams of hope in his earlier books. But in 1984 he seems to be saying that the future holds no prospect of brotherhood, but only of Big Brother, unless men can love something more than they love themselves; and he seems to doubt if this is possible. In any case, he demands *proof*. It is no use to tell him that you would give your life for your children, your country, your honor, and so forth. He wants to know if you would stick to it under torture. This may seem unreasonable, and perhaps it is an example of the strain of cussedness in him. But it is also an example, if an exaggerated one, of the remorseless honesty from which his work derives its rare vitality and its unmistakable touch of nobility.

And lays the sleek, estranging shield
Between the lover and his bride.
                            —From "St. Andrew's Day, 1935"

IN HIS ESSAY *Why I Write* Orwell tells us that, from early childhood, he always knew that when he grew up he was going to be a writer. He then goes on to say:

> Between the ages of about seventeen and twenty-four I tried to abandon the idea, but I did so with the consciousness that I was outraging my true nature and that sooner or later I should have to settle down and write books.

What he in fact did when he left school was to join the Indian Imperial Police in Burma. One obvious reason for doing this, instead of going on to a university, was to release his father from the necessity of supporting him, though another may well have been that he was under some inner compulsion to "outrage his true nature." But five years in Burma were enough to give him a violent detestation for imperialism, and he returned to Europe in 1927. At first he lived in Paris, writing stories which failed to achieve publication and which he later destroyed; and then, when he had no money left, he got a job as a dishwasher. After a few months of this he returned to England and lived in and around London as a tramp. Objectively, there can have been no necessity to do so. His prospects were not brilliant, but almost no one else in his place at that time would have sunk to sleeping on the floor in Paris kitchens and London workhouses.

He appears to have done this deliberately as a kind of penance or ablution to wash himself clean of the taint of imperialism.

> I had carried my hatred of oppression to extraordinary lengths. At that time failure seemed to me to be the only virtue. Every suspicion of self-advancement, even to "succeed" in life to the extent of making a few hundreds a year, seemed to me spiritually ugly, a species of bullying.—*The Road to Wigan Pier*

Nevertheless, his experience of the gutter did eventually become the subject of his first book, and there is no doubt that his impulse to write was so strong that he regarded all his experiences as potential copy. The Burmese experience gave him the material for his first novel, *Burmese Days* (1934), and also for the admirable essays, "Shooting an Elephant" and "A Hanging."

It also contributed very importantly to the development of his character and philosophy. He had been, as we have shown, a disaffected schoolboy with a strong "outsider" complex. But even in those days, as his schoolfellow Cyril Connolly observed, he was an unusually mature and responsible type of rebel; and there was a notable strain of conservatism in him to counterbalance his libertarian radicalism. The Burmese experience stimulated both the conservative and the anarchic strains in his character. In his wartime pamphlet, *The Lion and the Unicorn,* he compared the British people to a family in which there was a conspiracy of silence about the source of the family income, one of the main sources being, of course, the British Empire. And he was fond of reminding people —and more particularly the anti-imperialist, anti-militarist, or pacifist intellectuals—that it was the work of colonial officials that filled their pockets and the guns of the Navy that protected their skins. But in *Burmese Days* he shows colonialism on its last legs and the mood of the book is atrabilious. The British are hysterical and the Burmese are childish and corrupt.

However, in spite of the monotony of mood it was a remarkable first novel, solid and well-constructed and obviously the work of a writer determined to master his craft. The snobbish memsahib—the "scraggy old boiling fowl" Mrs. Lackersteen—feverishly husband-hunting for her frigid niece, and the forlorn hero with his disfiguring birthmark and his imprudent friendship with an Indian doctor challenge comparison with Somerset Maugham and E. M. Forster respectively, and do not come off too badly. But the style is heavily "literary" and it sometimes descends to cliché: "There was nothing that gave him quite so much pleasure as dragging a woman's name through mud." And there is something rather Anglo-Indian about the disparaging reference to an artist's technique "founded on dirty brushes," as if Orwell thought that a pukka artist parades every morning with shining palette and brushes trimmed.

Perhaps the most deeply felt thing in the book is the author's love-hate for the country of Burma, and some of the best writing is in the descriptive passages. For example:

> Some doves in a bamboo thicket kept up a dull droning noise, curiously appropriate to the heat—a sleepy sound, but with the sleepiness of chloroform rather than a lullaby.

But the main theme is the anachronism of the British Raj. The little group of officials and their wives are out on a limb; unappreciated at home, hating and hated by the local population, and getting on one another's nerves as they stew in their own juice in the jungle.

Orwell left Burma with a violent hatred of British Imperialism. Yet he was fairminded enough to write, only a few years later in his essay "Shooting an Elephant," that the British Empire "is a good deal better than the younger empires that are going to supplant it"; and to the end of his life he was scathing about the hypocrisy of the vociferously anti-imperialist left wing, which hushed up the fact that the British workers' relatively high standard of life was largely subsidized by the profits of empire:

> Quite largely, indeed, the workers were won over to socialism by being told that they were exploited, whereas the brute truth was that, in world terms, they were exploiters.—"Writers and Leviathan"

And again in his essay on Kipling:

> We all live by robbing Asiatic coolies and those of us who are "enlightened" all maintain that those coolies ought to be set free; but our standard of living, and hence our "enlightenment," demands that the robbery shall continue. A humanitarian is always a hypocrite, and Kipling's understanding of this is perhaps the crucial secret of his power to create telling phrases. It would be difficult to hit off the one-eyed pacifism of the English in fewer words than in the phrase "making mock of uniforms that guard you while you sleep."

Much could be said about this passage, but it is sufficient at this point to note that it might be construed as a kind of amends to his old colleagues of the Indian Imperial Police.

For some years after his return to England the strug-

gle to earn a living left Orwell little time to learn anything about politics. His first four books were written
in such time as he could spare from schoolteaching,
working in a bookshop, and reviewing. Not only *Down
and Out in Paris and London,* but the three novels
also, are to some extent autobiographical, although the
protagonist of the second novel, *A Clergyman's
Daughter,* is a young woman. This is not to its advantage, because Orwell singularly lacked the gift of identifying himself with the opposite sex, or indeed with
anyone outside himself. His later novel, *Coming up
for Air,* is somewhat exceptional, as we shall see, in
this and other respects; but, in general, Orwell was not
interested in psychology or in subtleties of character.
He understood Fielding but not Jane Austen, Dickens
but not Dostoevsky; and the values in his novels are
those of *Jack the Giant-Killer,* though he is too honest
not to show Jack getting terribly mauled.

TO SAY that Orwell could not enter into the characters
of people unlike himself and describe them from the
inside is not at all to say that he was bad at describing them. Dorothy, the clergyman's daughter, with her
patience and rectitude, her self-discipline and her
strong sense of duty, is a touching figure. Her appearance at the age of twenty-eight is described as follows:

> It was a thin, blonde, unremarkable kind of face, with
> pale eyes and a nose just a shade too long; if you
> looked closely you could see crow's feet around the
> eyes, and the mouth, when it was in repose, looked
> tired.

This might almost be a description of Orwell's own
face, and perhaps it was; though with his long, loose,
and yet somehow military figure, he could never have
been called unremarkable.

But Dorothy resembles her creator in more than appearance. Going up to the altar for Holy Communion she finds herself hoping that she will not have to take the chalice after the repulsive Miss Mayfill, with her yellow false teeth and "fringe of dark, dewy moustache." This repugnance, at such a moment, strikes her as a deadly sin and she contemplates forgoing the sacrament, but

> then it happened that she glanced sidelong, through the open south door. A momentary spear of sunlight had pierced the clouds. It struck downwards through the leaves of the limes, and a spray of leaves in the doorway gleamed with a transient, matchless green, greener than jade or emerald or Atlantic waters. . . . Somehow, because of the greenness of the leaves, it was again possible to pray. O all ye green things upon the earth, praise ye the Lord! She began to pray, ardently, joyfully, thankfully. The wafer melted upon her tongue. She took the chalice from her father, and tasted without repulsion, even with an added joy in this small act of self-abasement, the wet imprint of Miss Mayfill's lips on the silver rim.

Note the expression "self-abasement." Orwell himself was one of the most squeamish and easily disgusted of men. He went through life wincing at its small sordid horrors; and yet he went out of his way to sup more than his fill of them. Almost certainly it was not the fatigue, hunger and cold of the tramp's life, or of the trenches on the Aragon front, but the minor trials, such as drinking out of a shared cup or using a dirty latrine, that he found hardest to bear. (In *The Road to Wigan Pier* when he notices the dirty thumb marks on the cut bread and butter at breakfast he does not fail to remember that he had earlier seen the boarding-house proprietor holding a full chamber pot with his thumb well over the rim.)

In the novel, Dorothy loses her memory and finds herself alone and penniless in London, where she recapitulates Orwell's own experiences after his return from Paris. She joins a party of hop-pickers, begs at back doors, sleeps in the open in Trafalgar Square, and gets a starveling job as teacher in a horrible school. Finally she goes home again to continue housekeeping for her stingy father. And what has she learned from her experiences? Well, for one thing, she decides in future to make sure of taking the Communion chalice before Miss Mayfill. The sacrament itself no longer means anything to her, because she has lost her faith. The last thirty pages of the book, in which Orwell describes the position of a penniless clergyman's daughter who no longer believes, are so unpretentiously written that the reader may easily underrate the author's intellectual power. Dorothy has an argument with a hedonistic middle-aged debauchee, who wants to marry her, and totally fails to persuade him that loss of faith is a serious matter. "Even the loathsome platitudes of the pantheists," she reflects, "would be beyond his understanding."

Why does Orwell make Dorothy think pantheism "loathsome"? Perhaps because it still seems to her blasphemous to say that God is *everything*—including, for example, Miss Mayfill's pendulous underlip and dark, dewy moustache; but this is unlikely because, at this point in the book, Dorothy is as intelligent as Orwell himself and she does not call pantheism false or blasphemous, but platitudinous. A little later she reflects:

> Think of life as it really is, think of the *details* of life; and then think that there is no meaning in it, no purpose, no goal except the grave. . . . There was, she saw clearly, no possible substitute for faith; no pagan acceptance of life as sufficient to itself, no pantheistic

cheer-up stuff, no pseudo-religion of "progress" with visions of glittering Utopiae and ant-heaps of steel and concrete. It is all or nothing. Either life on earth is a preparation for something greater and more lasting, or it is meaningless, dark and dreadful.

It is the horrible *details* of life that she cannot stomach. But if you have sufficient money you can avoid or ignore a good many of these details. In fact, if you are comfortable enough the platitude that God is everything and everything is God is not so difficult to accept. And what makes it loathsome is not the platitudinousness but your own hypocrisy. You have not tried to find out if you can still believe it when you are uncomfortable. Would it still seem true if you were being tortured?

All or nothing might well have been Orwell's motto.

IN 1936 Orwell married Eileen O'Shaughnessy, a charming and intelligent woman, whose brother was a distinguished surgeon. In the same year he published *Keep the Aspidistra Flying*, his third novel, which describes the courtship and marriage of Gordon Comstock and Rosemary Waterlow. Like the others, this novel is to some extent autobiographical, although the hero is a travesty of Orwell himself. Gordon Comstock chucks up a "good" job in an advertising agency and becomes a seedy bookseller's assistant, writing poetry in his spare time. It is true that there is something heroic, and Orwellian, in his effort to renounce the struggle for money and success; but his public self-pity and "angry young man" tantrums are totally unlike Orwell. It makes him miserable to accept money from a rich friend, and it drives him to a frenzy when, on one occasion, the generous and long-suffering Rosemary has to supply the money for their tea and bus fares; and yet he is not above sponging on his impoverished and equally long-suffering sister. In the end he is a disastrously defeated rebel and returns to the advertising agency to write copy for a campaign to frighten the public into buying a deodorant for "P.P.," or smelly feet.

There are at least two reasons why this novel deserves close attention. In the first place, it marked the end of the first period of Orwell's writing. The year 1936 was a turning point in his career. And second, because of its points of similarity with 1984, the novel which ended his third and last period of writing. The motto of *Keep the Aspidistra Flying* is an "adaptation" of I Corinthians 13: "Though I speak with the tongues of men and angels, and have not money, I am become as a sounding brass or a tinkling cymbal" and so on, down to "And now abideth faith, hope, money, these three; but the greatest of these is money." One of the main themes of the book is that the hero's sex life is frustrated by his poverty—his *middle-class* poverty, because Orwell assumes that the working class have more spirit:

> Hats off to the factory lad who with fourpence in his pocket puts his girl in the family way! At least he's got blood and not money in his veins.

The first pages of the book are reminiscent of the beginning of Aldous Huxley's *Antic Hay* where the hero suffers agonies of boredom in Eton Chapel. The description of Gordon's work in the bookshop is very much in Huxley's style. But how differently it continues! In Orwell's novel there is no fantasy and not a great deal of wit; there is a kind of deadly and somehow impressive seriousness. In his feeble way, poor Gordon is *really* fighting against the power of money. And there is more to it than that, because there are complications which are also serious and profound.

His rebellion collapses when he has put Rosemary "in the family way" and realizes that he "would sooner cut his right hand off" than allow her to have an abortion. It is Rosemary's love and self-sacrifice that defeat him. But in addition to sabotaging his genuine rebellion she also saves him from something discreditable in himself—"an evil mutinous mood." (It is remarkable how often the word "evil" occurs in Orwell's prose: evil-smelling, evil-looking, etc. And "vile" is another favorite word.) In this mood Gordon is not so much a St. George fighting the money dragon as a sulky boy rejecting the inevitable conditions of life. It is true that the mood is partly excusable as a result of the sufferings of his struggle against worldy success. Like Orwell himself, he regarded any kind of success as a species of bullying; but one cannot help suspecting that the same mood contributed something, at the beginning, to his original and, in the main, creditable impulse of rebellion.

> One night the bugs came out of one of the cracks and marched across the ceiling two by two. He lay on his bed, his hands under his head, watching them with interest. Without regret, almost intentionally, he was letting himself go to pieces. At the bottom of all his feelings there was a sulkiness, a je m'en fous in the face of the world. Life had beaten him; but you can still beat life by turning your face away. Better to sink than rise. Down, down into the ghost-kingdom, the shadowy world where shame, effort, decency do not exist!

That is Gordon, and of course Orwell was a very different person. But I believe that there was in him, too, a touch of Ivan Karamazov. His criticism and invective were, for the most part, generous and sane; but there were moments, more particularly up to and including 1935, when they were inspired by the not entirely noble or admirable impulse "to give back his entrance ticket."

In 1936 when he wrote *The Road to Wigan Pier* (published 1937) there was a striking change, and *Keep the Aspidistra Flying* seems to have rid him of much of his accumulated bile. Except for *1984*, it is his bitterest book, though the three that preceded it were all in the same mood. In *Keep the Aspidistra Flying* the money god says, in effect: Obey me by getting a "good" (i.e. an immoral, anti-social and degrading) job and you can afford to have a baby. Disobey me, by writing poetry or doing any disinterested work, and you will have to forgo sex altogether, because no woman will go with a pauper; or if you do have the luck to find a generous girl, you will have to resort to contraceptives or abortion. Gordon disobeys, and becomes a pauper. But he is seduced by Rosemary, and since he will not use contraceptives—"the sleek estranging shield"—or allow her to resort to abortion, he is lost. He has no choice but to submit and become a respectable writer of advertising copy. But at least he may keep his baby, and even his opinions—provided he keeps them to himself.

In *1984*, however, Winston Smith and Julia are living under an even worse tyranny than money—an absolute, all-embracing totalitarianism. By daring to love one another and have a private life together, they put themselves outside every pale; and the only way back is through total submission, even in their inmost thoughts. But while Gordon is still a rebel his furtive and penurious expeditions to the country with Rosemary are remarkably like the brief escapade of Winston and Julia. Both Gordon and Winston feel prematurely old and moth-eaten and can hardly believe that any woman could love them. (Compare *Keep the Aspidistra Flying*, chapter 7, and *1984*, Part 2, chapter 2.) But Gordon, although he is aware of the misery of the unemployed and the down-trodden lower middle-class, is fighting mainly for his own freedom; and like Flory in *Burmese Days* he would probably think of freedom as sitting under the Parisian plane trees "drinking white wine and talking about Marcel Proust." Whereas Winston Smith is fighting, and knows he is fighting, not only for his own right to a private life and love but for the human consciousness and the freedom of the whole human race. *Keep the Aspidistra Flying*, therefore, is a narrower book in scope; but it is not shallow. Gordon's revulsion at the thought of killing his unborn baby is profoundly felt and profoundly described:

> For the first time he grasped, with the only kind of knowledge that matters, what they were really talking about. The words "a baby" took on a new significance. They did not mean any longer a mere abstract disaster, they meant a bud of flesh, a bit of himself, down there in her belly, alive and growing. His eyes met hers. They had a strange moment of sympathy such as they had never had before. For a moment he did feel that in some mysterious way they were one flesh . . . He knew then it was a dreadful thing they were contemplating—a blasphemy, if that word had any meaning.

THERE IS one weakness in *Keep the Aspidistra Flying* which almost disappeared from Orwell's later books, only to crop up again in *1984:* his unrealistic attitude toward the urban working class. Until he went to Lancashire in 1936 to obtain material for *The Road to Wigan Pier* he had had no special opportunity to learn anything about them. In Burma there were only coolies and in Paris and London he had mixed chiefly with down-and-outs and eccentrics. So it is not surprising that his references to the working class in his early novels should be somewhat stereotyped. But the stereotype is really that of the comic post-card—of which he was later to make such a brilliant study. Passing a pub and hearing the noise of singing, Gordon Comstock thinks of "prosperous plumbers" and imagines "twenty scarlet faces disappearing into pots of beer"; and a taxi driver is described as "a stout philosophic man with a weatherbeaten face and a knowing eye." In *The Road to Wigan Pier* Orwell rightly criticizes Shaw for introducing the working class into his plays only as figures of fun, "ready-made comic East Enders"; but unfortunately he himself shows a similar tendency with his clichés about scarlet faces and stout philosophers with knowing eyes; and if this seems hypercritical as a comment on *Keep the Aspidistra Flying* it will perhaps appear less so when we come to examine 1984.

The comic post-card motif appears again in Gordon's reflections on adultery:

> Commit adultery if you must, but at any rate have the decency to *call* it adultery. None of that American soul-mate slop. Have your fun and then sneak home, juice of the forbidden fruit dripping from your whiskers, and take the consequences. Cut-glass whisky decanters broken over your head, nagging, burnt meals, children crying, clash and thunder of embattled mothers-in-law.

Here of course the comic banality is intentional; and the defence of old-fashioned English lower middle-class conventionality against decadent modern "American soul-mate slop" is pleasantly characteristic of Orwell in his vigorous controversial mood.

BY 1936 Orwell had produced four books, and from 1934 onward he had been able to scrape a difficult living by his pen, without having to support himself by other work. He was thirty-three, and although far from being an established writer he had received some favorable notice. Sir Compton Mackenzie, no mean judge of the naturalistic novel, had been enthusiastic. Writing of *Down and Out in Paris and London, Burmese Days,* and *A Clergyman's Daughter,* he said:

> I have no hesitation in asserting that no "realistic" writer during the last five years has produced three volumes which can compare in directness, vigour, courage and vitality with these three volumes from the pen of Mr. George Orwell.

But Orwell's straightforward naturalistic style was out of fashion in those days, and not many of the influential critics were able to recognize the strong and honest intelligence and the promise of originality and power. Perhaps this was partly because his solidly constructed books, although packed with matter, did not have the grace and charm and humor that were to adorn so much of his later work.

Another characteristic of his first four books is a certain simplicity, which is really a form of modesty and humility. He was the industrious apprentice to literature, the conscientious aspirant to public favor. In his first appearance in print, with *Down and Out in Paris and London,* he probably counted upon the unusual subject matter to compensate for his inexperience as a writer. And there is something ingenuous in the chapter of *A Clergyman's Daughter* which describes the heroine's night in Trafalgar Square. It is Orwell's first and last piece of "experimental" writing, and by introducing it in the middle of a conventional novel he seems, as it were, to be putting his cards on the table. A more pretentious or calculating young writer would have sent it by itself to some Anglo-Franco-American *avant garde* magazine. But Orwell was never attracted to coteries, and if he became interested in a coterie writer he always wanted to explain him and make him accessible to a wider audience.

There is an interesting passage in his essay "Why I Write" in which he lists what he considers to be the four main motives which animate all writers of prose. They are: sheer egoism, aesthetic enthusiasm, historical impulse, and political purpose. He allows that they are mixed in different proportions in different writers and in the same writer at different times, but it is significant and characteristic that he puts sheer egoism first and has most to say about it. By aesthetic enthusiasm he means "perception of beauty in the external world, or, on the other hand, in words and their right arrangement"; by political purpose, "desire to push the world in a certain direction, to alter other people's idea of the kind of society they should strive after." He emphasizes that no book can ever be genuinely free from political bias because even "the opinion that art should have nothing to do with politics is itself a political attitude." He considers that he himself is by temperament a writer in whom political purpose would tend to be weaker than the three other motives—"in a peaceful age I might have written ornate or merely descriptive books"—but circumstances have forced him into becoming "a sort of political pamphleteer." All this is perceptive and true and, as so often with Orwell, there is a great deal more in it than appears at first sight.

The writer's egoism he describes as follows: "Desire to seem clever, to be talked about, to be remembered after death, to get your own back on grown-ups who snubbed you in childhood, etc., etc." He points out that writers share these characteristics with scientists, artists, politicians, etc., "in short, with the whole top crust of humanity" and continues:

The great mass of human beings are not acutely selfish. After the age of about thirty they abandon individual ambition—in many cases, indeed, they almost abandon the sense of being individuals at all—and live chiefly for others, or simply smothered under drudgery. But there is also the minority of gifted, wilful people who are determined to live their own lives to the end, and writers belong in this class.

Once again this is obviously true, but in Orwell's case the self-assertion and desire for success were strikingly honest and innocent; and when he finally achieved best-seller status with *Animal Farm* and 1984 his success was, among other things, the deserved reward of a writer who had labored conscientiously all his life to be understood and appreciated, as Dickens was, not merely by intellectuals and literary critics, but by the great unintellectual public.

IT WOULD BE convenient and tidy to be able to say that in 1936 Eric Blair disappeared and was replaced by "George Orwell." But in fact his first book, in 1933, was signed Orwell although he continued to sign as Eric Blair in *The Adelphi* until 1935. Why did he take a pen name? The reasons he gave were characteristic and quaint. On one occasion he told me that it gave him an unpleasant feeling to see his real name in print because "how can you be sure your enemy won't cut it out and work some sort of black magic on it?" Whimsy, of course; but even Orwell's genuine streak of old-fashioned conventionality sometimes bordered on whimsy and you could not always be quite certain if he was serious or not. It would have been quite like him to insist, as Gordon Comstock did, upon having an aspidistra in the house.

Another reason he gave for the change was his dislike of the Scottish associations of the name Blair. This also seems whimsical, but on the other hand there is no doubt that he *did* like the East Anglian associations of the name of the river Orwell. As to his pretended dislike of Scotland, he later overcame it to the extent of making his home there. But it is a fact that he considered the cult of Scottishness as an affectation of the English, and this prejudice dated back to his preparatory school days. It had irritated him to hear richer boys boasting about their fathers' grouse moors and talking familiarly of salmon fishing, deer stalking and ghillies; and from this he appears to have deduced that the prevalence in England of names like Donald and Malcolm and Douglas was a result of snobbishness; middle-class people aping the fashions of the rich.

4 SOCIALISM

And little fat men shall ride them.
          —From "A Happy Vicar I Might Have Been"

IN THE EARLY NINETEEN-THIRTIES a wave of hysterical Russia-worship swept through the English intelligentsia, washing many of them into the Communist Party and leaving many more on the brink of it as fellow travelers. This outbreak of hysteria was in part a release for the genuine and justified feelings of impotence and shame induced by the spectacle of mass unemployment. Between the two wars the lives of a considerable proportion of Britain's industrial workers, especially in the north, were paralyzed by this long-drawn-out and seemingly interminable horror, and it is no wonder that the more sensitive intellectuals found the sight of it unbearable. Their hysteria was also in part a reaction to the growing menace of Hitler.

Unfortunately, both as a release of feeling and as a political reaction it was unhealthy—most often futile and sometimes mischievous. Orwell, who must have been almost unique among the intellectuals of that time in his knowledge of the facts of extreme poverty, was one who kept his head. He was never intoxicated by the revolutionary toasts and dialectical-materialist cocktails which flowed like water wherever the progressive intellectuals foregathered; and it is worth recalling the extraordinary and hysterical background against which he stands out. Considering how many future literary professors and pundits were among the most fiery "revolutionaries," it is strange that this period should be so badly documented, at least in England. In America, perhaps partly because of the Hiss case, something has been written: Mr. Trilling's brilliant *The Middle of the Journey*, for example, and some illuminating reminiscences by Miss Mary McCarthy.* But if I did not personally remember them I should hardly know where to find a record of the insane theories advocated in England by Leftist intellectuals and fellow-traveling professional and business men who, apart from their political hysteria, seemed to be sane and sometimes even talented and reliable and responsible individuals. In brief, what they appeared to want—though clearly there was some sort of mental blockage or, as Orwell was later to call it, "doublethink" which prevented them from understanding what they said—was a breakdown of law and order which would produce a situation in Britain comparable to that in Petrograd in 1917. Parliamentary democracy would be abolished; all property owners would be expropriated; the economic life of the country would be brought to a standstill and then restarted on the lines of government by "soviets" or "workers' councils." I remember a man who is today an eminent pundit in the literary establishment vehemently informing me as editor of the *Adelphi* that if I did not bring the magazine out unequivocally for "the Revolution" within a week or two I should be too late.

* Almost the only serious attempt to document the English thirties happens also to be by an American, Dr. Neal Wood (*Communism and British Intellectuals*); but although he covers a lot of ground he hardly does more than scratch the surface of the deeper moral and psychological problems involved.

When I asked for some evidence that a revolutionary situation existed, he spoke of the mutinous state of mind of the rank and file of the Guards regiments who do duty at Buckingham Palace.

What is more extraordinary than these fantasies is the fact that otherwise intelligent people should have succeeded in persuading themselves, even by means of doublethink, that a highly industrialized Western country in the 1930's, totally dependent upon a complicated international trading system, could improve its condition by disrupting its entire political, social and economic life and installing overnight a new and inconceivable method of government by groups of workers in "field, factory and mine," as the phrase went. There were others, of course, who were not so naive. They merely advocated a "Popular Front" policy—an alliance between Liberals, Socialists and Communists—which was intended, whether they understood this or not, to bring communism to power and destroy its allies by the subtler methods which were later to be successfully employed in Czecho-Slovakia and elsewhere. But whatever the policy, nearly all the bright young progressives claimed to be "revolutionaries."

The explanation, and to some extent the excuse, for all these aberrations was, of course, that nerves and consciences were tormented both by the aggressions of Hitler abroad and by the inability of orthodox politicians at home to deal with the hideous problem of unemployment. But, excusable or not, there was something ludicrous and discreditable about the contrast between the verbal ferocity and the practical nullity of the bourgeois revolutionaries. They did nothing much except talk or write poems; very few sacrifices were made or dangers incurred. People whose socialist convictions had not sprouted overnight and who knew the facts of political life were often embarrassed by the crowd of new and excitable allies. As R. H. Tawney put it, invitations to join tiger hunts were being issued by people with whom one would hesitate to go rabbit shooting.*

Orwell was not one of these. Although no politician, his experiences among the down-and-outs had taught him something about the facts of life. Up to about 1930 he had remained a sort of Bohemian tory-an-archist. "On the whole," he was to write in a biographical preface to the Ukrainian translation of *Animal Farm*, "up to 1930 I didn't consider myself a socialist. By nature I had as yet no clearly defined political views. I became a socialist more out of disgust with the oppressed and neglected life of the poorer section of the industrial workers than out of any theoretical understanding of a planned society." And even by the end of 1935, as he tells us in *Why I Write*, he had not yet reached "a firm decision." When Orwell did reach decisions they were firm ones.

In 1936 he obtained a commission from a publisher to study and report on the living conditions of unemployed miners in Lancashire and Yorkshire; and in the book that resulted we can see him in the process of making up his mind. This book, *The Road to Wigan Pier*, was something of a sensation, even to those who knew him well. Up till then he had been groping, and it would have been possible to read *Keep the Aspidistra Flying* as a sign that he was in a cul-de-sac. But in *The Road to Wigan Pier*, besides revealing what he

* It is of some sociological interest that there was a second wave of red hysteria in France in the 1940's. The German occupation seems to have done to the French intellectuals what the prolonged economic crisis did to the English. The chief difference was that in France some of the more intelligent victims of hysteria made a much more serious and prolonged attempt to intellectualize it. For years after the war, J.-P. Sartre was trying to combine existentialist theory with fellow-traveling practice—if, indeed, he is not still doing so.

had seen in the mining towns of the north, he began to reveal his true self. The book is in two parts, the first being a straightforward account of what he saw in the mines and in the working-class homes he visited. It is in the second part that the fireworks begin, when he discusses the remedy for the state of affairs he has been describing. This remedy is socialism, by which he seems to mean a planned society, with private ownership abolished or greatly restricted, and democratically governed in the interests of the majority of the people by their elected representatives. But Orwell was no political theorist. What he does is to give a sketch of his own intellectual development up to the time he became a socialist, followed by an account of his disappointment on meeting other middle-class socialists, of the unsatisfactory state of contemporary socialism, and of how it should be remedied. The first part of the book is less controversial, but is still today of documentary interest. Orwell knew enough about poverty to be an unusually good observer of life on the unemployment dole, and his independence of mind begins to appear even in his factual reporting. The radio and newspapers, with their up-to-the-minute results of sporting events, are described as "the queer spectacle of modern electrical science showering miracles upon people with empty bellies." He understands why most of the unemployed do not eat dull, sensible meals but prefer to waste their money on a bite of something "tasty." He understands the "healthy instinct" by which they reject what passes for education nowadays, and he refrains from critizing the apparent selfishness of the unemployed man who never lifts a finger to help his overburdened wife with the housework. "I believe that they [the women], as well as the men, feel that a man would lose his manhood if, merely because he was out of work, he developed into a 'Mary Ann.' "

Obviously this kind of detached and realistic observation was liable to get Orwell into trouble both with reactionaries and with progressives; and in the second part of the book he made sure of it. Socialism, so the argument runs, is the only remedy for the shameful and intolerable conditions he has described, and why is this not obvious to the great majority of middle-class as well as working-class people—since both have so much to gain by voting for it? The answer is that there is something badly wrong with socialists themselves. And at this point, carried away by the exuberance of his new-found faith and purpose in life, his arguments become, sometimes, brilliant but, sometimes, wildly unfair. We will begin by examining the unfair ones.

Ignoring the fact that the Labour Party, the trade unions, and the co-operative movement were mainly the creation of working-class socialists, he speaks of socialism as if it were a creed monopolized by middle-class cranks and eccentrics, and more particularly by his own personal *bêtes noires*: "fruit-juice drinkers, nudists, sandal-wearers, sex-maniacs, Quakers, 'Nature Cure' quacks, pacifists and feminists." That is a typical list of Orwell's favorite Aunt Sallies, "who come flocking towards the smell of 'progress' like blue-bottles to a dead cat." Then, having pilloried his official comrades, he turns upon the official enemy and we find Roman Catholics in the dock. They have "an attitude of mind that can make even food and drink an occasion for religious intolerance." G. K. Chesterton, for example, is continually denouncing tea and praising beer. But if Orwell is free to denounce fruit juice on every other page, why should Chesterton be forbidden to denounce tea? In reality, Orwell and Chesterton had certain attitudes in common; and when the one denounced fruit juice and the other denounced tea, what they were both implicitly condemning was an assumption of superiority on the part of people who do not share the traditional (and supposedly alcoholic) tastes of the common man. It was the assumption of superiority rather than the nature of the liquid that they objected to.

Nevertheless, a not unsympathetic critic of Orwell has deduced from these passages that he was fundamentally a believer in conformity as well as an equalitarian. In *Partisan Review* (Winter, 1960) this critic, Mr. Richard Wollheim, notes that Orwell seems to have disliked "crankiness, affectation, perversion, 'softness,' aestheticism" and goes on to say:

> I don't think that he would have regarded it as any great breach of liberty to crowd these things out of society—not to suppress them, mind you, but to crowd them out, to sweep them under the carpet.

It is obviously true that in Orwell's *ideal* society people would not be cranky, affected, perverted or "soft"; though it is going too far to accuse him of anti-aestheticism. But in any *real* society he would certainly have been up in arms against the slightest injustice or discrimination against any minority, however cranky or freakish.

Yet he did exhibit a prejudice against sandals, fruit juice, etc. But liberal-minded people who feel upset by this should beware. No human being is always perfectly consistent and, moreover, most of us are much more intolerant and conformist than we believe. When we think that we have shaken off our prejudices we have often merely exchanged them unconsciously for new ones; and it happens to be precisely one of Orwell's merits that he so clearly perceived this fact. Indeed, he was in some danger of being called a crank himself because of his punctilious championship of eccentric and unpopular minorities. But it remains true that he does exhibit in *The Road to Wigan Pier* a certain intolerance for the sort of people he considered cranks and freaks, and he could only have answered this charge by saying that he attacked them because they seemed to him to monopolize the socialist movement and hinder its growth.

AS A POLITICIAN in the strict sense of the word, Orwell cannot be said to have developed toward greater realism with the passage of time. True, the denunciations of fruit juice and sandals were supplemented by more useful denunciations of rubber truncheons and concentration camps. But these were German or Russian phenomena, and the enemy on the home front continued to be seen too often as a comic post-card figure. Indeed, it would hardly be a misrepresentation to depict the weakness of Orwell's view of British politics as follows: Scene—the Stock Exchange, a groggy-looking, heavily fissured concrete skyscraper, with evil faces at every window—a Rolls Royce drives up and out of it there emerges a fat old woman, swathed in mink, cuddling a Pekingese, and with a protruding black velvet posterior— She waddles into the building— Meanwhile, a procession of socialists straggles by, bearded, sandaled, spectacled, holding banners proclaiming "Down with the Army and the Navy! Down with the Demon Drink! Up with Free Love and Fruit Juice!"

But at his best he was much more realistic, and indeed a better Marxist than the theoretical pundits of socialism and communism. Note, for example, the difference he discovers between comic post-cards and the twopenny weekly papers. In comic post-cards "there are no anti-trade union jokes. Broadly speaking, anyone with much over or much under £5 a week is regarded as laughable. . . . Unlike the twopenny weekly papers, comic post-cards are not the product of

any great monopoly company, and evidently they are
not regarded as having any importance in forming public opinion. There is no sign in them of any attempt to
induce an outlook acceptable to the ruling class" (The
Art of Donald McGill). As regard the twopenny
weeklies he reaches the opposite conclusion.

These two unique and remarkable studies are among
Orwell's most original contributions to sociology and
politics. Neither before him nor after him have there
been any intellectuals capable of studying social phenomena from his peculiar and rewarding angle of vision.

DURING THE WAR the comparatively high spirits that
sustained Orwell from 1936 to 1939 seem to have begun to evaporate, and his socialist polemics became
somewhat strained and shrill. In his wartime booklet
The Lion and the Unicorn it appears that he believed
it to be not only desirable but necessary and possible
that some socialist leader of a Cromwellian type—Sir
Stafford Cripps or, perhaps, Mr. Aneurin Bevan—
should precipitate a drastic social and economic revolution cither before the end of the war or immediately
after it. What in fact happened was that a moderate
Labour government carried through after the war a
number of social security and welfare measures which
went somewhat further, though not very much, than a
Conservative government would have been prepared to
go. And the failure to make a radical Cromwellian up-
heaval has not, so far, produced the disastrous alterna-
tives he foresaw. The distressed industrial areas which
Orwell visited in 1936 are today much more prosperous and the people in them hardly see themselves as
an oppressed and neglected class. But for all that, Orwell's main point in *The Road to Wigan Pier* is as
timely today as it was twenty-five years ago. His criti-

cism of the selfishness of capitalism, or the old lady in the Rolls Royce, is merely one form of a perennially valid criticism of human nature. People *are* selfish, and they like to hold on to what they have got. But his criticism of the socialism of Wells and Shaw is still of peculiar and special relevance to the semi-socialist or state-capitalist societies of the contemporary Western world. And it is the best part of the book. When he drops the fruit-juice drinkers and nudists and goes after the big game Orwell really comes into his own.

We hear something that is excessively rare in modern literature, something that had hardly been heard in England since D. H. Lawrence's death in 1930, and was hardly to be heard again after Orwell's in 1950: the voice of a man with a mind of his own, with something in his mind, and speaking his mind. Not the academic and cagey accents of a literary pundit, nor the suave tones of a public relations expert, nor the phonographic rigmarole of a party-liner, but the voice of an independent individual who saw with his own eyes and knew what he thought and how to say it. The rarity of the phenomenon was attested by the sensation it caused.

Here was a former Public-School boy and Empire builder advocating socialism, but without kowtowing to Marx or Stalin or apologizing for his own accent and manners; and, moreover, making fun of other middle-class socialists, criticizing sacred institutions like Wells, Shaw and the Webbs, and blaspheming against *The New Statesman*. Worse still, he not only confessed to having grown up with the illusion that working class people smell but accused other left-wing intellectuals of clinging to bourgeois social prejudices of their own. How often, he pertinently asked, do they marry out of their own class? He asserted that they were out of touch with the common man and that they

constituted, in their own persons, the chief reason why
large sections of the middle class were hostile to socialism, which they might otherwise be persuaded to
accept:

> The ordinary man may not flinch from a dictatorship
> of the proletariat, if you offer it tactfully; offer him a
> dictatorship of the prigs, and he gets ready to fight.

But his main point is much more fundamental. The
biggest reason for the failure of socialist propaganda,
he says, is that it takes too low a view of human nature; and this, of course, is at least as true, if not truer,
of the semi-socialist philosophies which are in vogue
today all over the world:

> They have never made it clear that the essential aims of
> socialism are justice and liberty. With their eyes glued
> to economic facts, they have proceeded on the assump-
> tion that man has no soul, and explicitly or implicitly
> they have set up the goal of a materialistic Utopia.

William Morris, with whom Orwell had several
points in common besides a clear and spare and mas-
culine prose style, might or might not have been sur-
prised to read this criticism of the movement he helped
to found. But it was a later generation of socialists that
Orwell was criticizing, and they have seldom had a
more advised and level-headed critic. No one knew
better than he that machinery has come to stay, and
that without it civilization must remain the monopoly
of a privileged few ("We all live by robbing Asiatic
coolies"). In so far as materialism makes sense, he was
a materialist. "How right the working classes are in
their materialism!" he wrote in "Looking Back on the
Spanish War." "How right they are to realise that the
belly comes before the soul, not in the scale of values
but in point of time!" His theme is that whether machinery leads to a degradation or to an improvement of

life will depend upon the motives behind our use of it.
Machinery regarded as a means is more or less neutral
—though there is one passage where he faces the possibility that the dominance of the machine may turn
out to be harmful in one way or another to *every* human capacity. What he chiefly fears, however, in *The
Road to Wigan Pier* (later he began to fear something
even worse) is that the end we have deliberately
chosen is to make the world safe for "little fat men."
He knows, of course, that to speak contemptuously of
little fat men is to invite the charge of hypocrisy. It
seems to imply a bleak, unrealistic, muscular ideal of
asceticism, austerity, and work for work's sake. But in
reality who wants to work harder than he need? Who
does not want life to be easy and comfortable? "We're
soft—for God's sake let's stay soft." This, as he says,
appears to be realistic, but it is really an evasion, because "it fails to make clear what we mean when we
say that we 'want' this or that. . . . I don't 'want' to
cut down my drinking, to pay my debts, to take enough
exercise, to be faithful to my wife, etc., etc., but in another and more permanent sense I do want these
things, and perhaps in the same sense I want a civilisation in which 'progress' is not definable as making
the world safe for little fat men."

And here he has to meet another obvious criticism.
Progress in a machine civilization is *not* the achievement of lazy fat little men; it calls not only for intel-
lect but also for courage of the highest order. In reply
to this he admits that the first men who went up in
aeroplanes must have been superlatively brave and
that it must still require an exceptionally good nerve
to be a pilot. But he points out that the *objective* is
still the same:

Finally—this is the objective, though it may never
quite be reached—you will get an aeroplane whose

pilot needs no more skill or courage than a baby needs
in its perambulator. . . . A machine evolves by becoming more efficient, that is, more fool-proof; hence the
objective of mechanical progress is a fool-proof world—
which may or may not mean a world inhabited by fools.
Mr. Wells would probably retort that the world can
never become fool-proof, because, however high a standard of efficiency you have reached, there is always some
greater difficulty ahead. For example (this is Mr. Wells'
favourite idea—he has used it in goodness knows how
many perorations), when you have got this planet of
ours perfectly into trim, you start upon the enormous
task of reaching and colonising another. But this is
merely to push the objective into the future; the objective itself remains the same. . . . In tying yourself to
the idea of mechanical efficiency, you tie yourself to
the ideal of softness. But softness is repulsive; and thus
all progress is seen to be a frantic struggle towards an
objective which you hope and pray will never be
reached. Now and again, but not often, you meet somebody who grasps that what is usually called progress
also entails what is usually called degeneracy, and who
is nevertheless in favour of progress. Hence the fact that
in Mr. Shaw's Utopia a statue was erected to Falstaff,
as the first man who ever made a speech in favour of
cowardice.

To the argument that in a completely mechanized
world people would be free, at last, to devote all their
time to creative work, Orwell's answer is implicit in
his criticism of the "Men Like Gods" theory:

It is assumed that such qualities as strength, courage,
generosity, etc., will be kept alive because they are
comely qualities and necessary attributes of a full human being. Presumably, for instance, the inhabitants of
Utopia would create artificial dangers in order to exercise their courage, and do dumb-bell exercises to harden
muscles which they would never be obliged to use.

This later becomes "saving one's soul by fretwork" and Orwell points out that the champion of progress becomes in the last analysis a champion of such anachronisms as the Tudor Tea Shoppe. This is all very bright and lively, but in the end Orwell admits that the argument is becoming academic, since everyone knows that, for better *and* worse, the machine has come to stay. He drops the subject with the sensible last word that "the machine has got to be accepted, but it is probably better to accept it rather as one accepts a drug—that is, grudgingly and suspiciously." After which he returns, rather perfunctorily, to the immediate problem of strengthening socialism to meet the fascist threat.

ONE THING that cannot be adequately conveyed in any attempt to summarize the argument of *The Road to Wigan Pier* is its wonderfully debonair and pungent style; and it is almost equally difficult to do justice to the real strength of Orwell's argument. He was far from being the old familiar *laudator temporis acti*. He was much more intelligent than the average reactionary or the average progressive because he understood so clearly that the fundamental social problem is the problem of incentive.* As he put it in "The Art of Donald McGill":

Society has always to demand a little more from human beings than it will get in practice. . . . I never read the

* Fourteen years later, in 1950, Arnold Toynbee was to write: "It looked as if the regimentation imposed by industrial technology might be taking the life out of the pre-industrial spirit of private enterprise. . . . The ultimate question therefore seemed to be whether there was some alternative source of psychic energy. . . . If mechanisation spelled regimentation, and if this regimentation had taken the spirit out of an industrial working class and out of a middle class in succession, was it possible for any human hands to handle the almighty machine with impunity?"—*A Study of History*, abridged ed., II, 338

proclamations of generals before battle, the speeches of führers and prime ministers, the solidarity songs of public schools and Left Wing political parties, national anthems, Temperance tracts, papal encyclicals and sermons against gambling and contraception, without seeming to hear in the background a chorus of raspberries from all the millions of common men to whom these high sentiments make no appeal. Nevertheless the high sentiments always win in the end, leaders who offer blood, toil, tears and sweat always get more out of their followers than those who offer safety and a good time. When it comes to the pinch, human beings are heroic.

Orwell knew that human beings are heroic, because he was heroic himself. Immediately after finishing *The Road to Wigan Pier* he was to prove it again in the Spanish civil war, while the vast majority of his left-wing critics stayed at home and made speeches. But before leaving *The Road to Wigan Pier* it must be emphasized again that the chief value of the book is not its contribution to the socialism-versus-fascism controversy of the nineteen-thirties but its far-sighted warning of dangers which in those days had scarcely appeared above the horizon. He saw that a planned society with the economic profit-motive eliminated would not necessarily be a free or a just society. It might easily be a slave state with well-fed and contented slaves. Later he was to foresee a similar state in which the slaves were not even well fed—a society of oppressed animals ruled by pigs. But in 1937 his imagination did not go beyond the comfortable slave state of Aldous Huxley's *Brave New World* and, in the long run, the only way to safeguard a socialist society against that sort of degeneration, he said, was to revive the underlying socialist ideals of justice and liberty.

It is still possible to argue that Orwell's prophecy

of a world safe for little fat men was premature, since
the majority of the world's population is still far from
the state in which they could afford to forget that
"the belly comes before the soul." But as regards the
Western world, and probably Russia also, it may be
later than we think. British politicians have been
promising to double our standard of living in twenty-
five years; Americans are exhorted to over-spend; and
Russians are boasting that they will soon be richer
than Americans. So, if we don't have a war, what do
we propose to do with all our wealth? Help the Asians
and Africans to become as rich as ourselves? And what
then? Colonize the moon? And what then?

> Once Socialism is in a way to being established, those
> who can see through the swindle of "progress" will
> probably find themselves resisting. In fact, it is their
> special function to do so. In the machine-world they
> have got to be a sort of permanent opposition, which
> is not the same thing as being an obstructionist or a
> traitor.—*The Road to Wigan Pier*.

Up to now, therefore, Orwell's criticism of modern
tendencies is not so much moral as aesthetic ("pour-
ing European civilisation down the sink at the com-
mand of Marxist prigs," "a sort of Lyons Corner
House lasting *in saecula saeculorum* and getting big-
ger and noisier all the time," and so on). It is only
when he is discussing the present (fascism, unemployment, inequality) that the criticism is primarily moral.
But what he saw in Spain was to change his estimate
of modern tendencies.

5 WAR

No bomb that ever burst
Shatters the crystal spirit.
—From "The Italian Soldier Shook My Hand"

THE INVASION OF LITERATURE by politics was bound to happen, and no one nowadays could devote himself to literature as single-mindedly as Joyce or Henry James—so Orwell asserted in 1948; and a year earlier he had written that on looking through his own work he saw that it was invariably when he lacked a *political* purpose that he wrote lifeless books. Looking back through his work in 1960 can we endorse this judgment? Or does it appear that a promising novelist was lost when Orwell turned to writing about socialism in *The Road to Wigan Pier?*

It is not true that his early novels were lifeless; but it is true that his writing entered a new and more lively phase when he became a socialist. Nevertheless, he did not abandon literature for politics. He combined the two. After 1936 he was to write one more admirable novel and a number of important literary essays; and his two last, and most famous, books were also works of fiction, though they are political fables rather than novels. But one of the best of all his books, *Homage to Catalonia* (1938), in which he describes his experiences in the Spanish civil war, is largely a factual report—although it is certainly also a work of art.

Orwell's ostensible reason for going to Spain in the winter of 1936 was to report the war for a London socialist weekly. He found Barcelona still in the exciting aftermath of the Anarchist counterrevolution against Franco; and it was not likely, being the man he was, when he saw the recruiting stations and the ragged youths and boys enlisting in the militias, that he would refrain from joining them. Being politically innocent and inexperienced, the fact that he found himself in a "Trotskyist" unit seemed to him of no particular significance. Was it not a part of the socialist working-class militia? One of the major themes of *Homage to Catalonia* is how he learned, and by the hardest way, the truth about Communist politics.

If his going to the north of England to report on the unemployed had been one of the turning points in his career, the discovery of the real nature of Russian communism was one of the major revelations to which it led him.

BUT THERE IS another even more important theme in *Homage to Catalonia* and it is developed in the first words of the book:

> In the Lenin Barracks in Barcelona, the day before I joined the militia, I saw an Italian militiaman standing in front of the officers' table.

After a brief description of the man he continues:

> I hardly know why, but I have seldom seen anyone— any man, I mean—to whom I have taken such an immediate liking. While they were talking round the table some remark brought it out that I was a foreigner. The Italian raised his head and said quickly:
> "Italiano?"

I answered in my bad Spanish: "No, Ingles. Y tu?"
   "Italiano."
As we went out he stepped across the room and gripped
my hand very hard. Queer, the affection you can feel
for a stranger! It was as though his spirit and mine had
momentarily succeeded in bridging the gulf of language
and tradition and meeting in utter intimacy.

He never saw the man again, and that is the last
time he is mentioned in the book, though he is referred to again very poignantly seven years later in the
essay "Looking back on the Spanish War." The significance of this incident may not be immediately obvious, but before discussing it we must look at the
book as a whole. It is, in the main, a story of disillusionment, muddle, persecution and danger, relieved by
some incidents of heroism among which the most
striking, though Orwell does not perceive the fact, are
supplied by himself and his wife. She had come to
Spain to work in the party offices in Barcelona of the
"Trotskyist" party in whose militia he was fighting.
This party was the P.O.U.M. and it was, in fact, not
Trotskyist although it was bitterly anti-Stalinist; it was
led by a small group of doctrinaire Marxists and was
liquidated when the Communists became the strong-
est party in the government, in June, 1937. Its suppression was accompanied by murders and wholesale ar-
rests and imprisonments, while the Communist press
in Spain, and in London, Paris and New York as-
sailed it with accusations of treachery and even of being a Fifth Column in the pay of Franco. At this
crisis Orwell, who was recovering from a wound (he
had been shot through the neck by a fascist sniper
while fighting in "Franco's Fifth Column"), and also
his wife, behaved with extraordinary courage and self-
lessness—postponing their escape to France in spite
of the imminent danger of arrest and attempting the

impossible to secure the release of an imprisoned comrade. Orwell thus found himself in the position of being one of the very few articulate people who were able to disprove from personal knowledge the slanderous lies written about his fellow militiamen by Communist journalists in newspaper offices thousands of miles from Spain. No doubt his experiences in Barcelona in 1937 contributed importantly to the preoccupation about the falsification of history which he developed so elaborately in 1984.

But the chapters in which he tries to rescue the truth about the Spanish war from Communist and Fascist historians are only a small part of the book, and most of it is a lively account of the training of militiamen, life on the Aragon front, the experience of being wounded, and his escape to France with the political police on his heels. In spite of all the horrors, it is predominantly a gay book, written almost in the style of a schoolboy's letter: "It was not bad fun in a way" (this comes in the middle of an account of a night attack) and "If there is one thing I hate more than another it is a rat running over me in the darkness. However, I had the satisfaction of catching one of them a good punch that sent him flying." His language is often commonplace, but the whole book is written with an élan and vigor which place it alongside David Jones' highly self-conscious and elaborately "written" masterpiece, *In Parenthesis*, among this century's few readable pieces of war literature. The first essential in literature is to have something interesting to say—which may be news to certain contemporary schools of literary criticism.

CONSIDERING that the greater part of his time in Spain was passed in the remote Aragonese mountains amid the day-to-day preoccupations of trench warfare, his grasp of the general situation in Spain is remarkable. And in spite of his natural bias towards the point of view of his own comrades, his view of the Anarchist-Communist controversy behind the Republican lines is reasonably balanced and objective. (His own group, the P.O.U.M., was small and independent, but it counted as an ally of the Anarchists.) He clearly perceived two essential points. First, that Anarchism is a sort of Spanish working class substitute for religious faith. "To the Spanish people, at any rate in Catalonia and Aragon, the Church was a racket pure and simple. And possibly Christian belief was replaced to some extent by Anarchism, whose influence is widely spread and which undoubtedly has a religious tinge." And second, that anarchist principles and methods are incompatible with the efficient prosecution of a war. (". . . such things as individual liberty and a truthful press are simply not compatible with military efficiency.")

So what? The Anarchists and the P.O.U.M. insisted that the social revolution and the war were interdependent and that to postpone the revolution until after the war would be to lose both. The Communists, on the other hand, allied themselves with the Liberal bourgeoisie and pressed for a strong centralized government, insisting that the successful prosecution of the war must be the first objective and that Anarchist fads about equality between officers and men, and workers' control of factories, etc., were an obstacle to the war effort.

Although Orwell admits the force of the Communists' argument, he cannot bring himself to accept the consequences of accepting it. He points out, very justly, that Communists everywhere had for years been denouncing parliamentary democracy as a swindle and that they had now turned about and were allying themselves with Liberal parliamentarians, while appealing to the European working class for support for a respectable Spanish democracy. This was obviously inconsistent, but whether it was done in good faith, as the most hopeful tactics for winning the war, it is hard to say. The role of the Communists or, more accurately, of Russia in the Spanish civil war is nothing if not enigmatic. Russia's support of the Republic was not impressively weighty; and Communist policy in Spain was carried through with savage unscrupulousness, and ended in military disaster. And the French, American, and British working classes looked on apathetically. Yet, for all this, it is hard to agree with Orwell's suggestion that an appeal to the workers of the world in the name of a revolutionary and anticlerical Spain would have met with a better response than the one that was actually made in the name of a democratic and respectable Spain.

The fact is that in Spain Orwell came up once more against the problem of Don Quixote and Sancho Panza—though in any case he brought it along with him. "When it comes to the pinch, human beings are heroic." But, perverse creatures that we are, we prefer to avoid the pinch; and Orwell never quite reconciled himself to this fact. Four years after his return from Spain—in London under the German bombs—he wrote two essays for Victor Gollancz's book *The Betrayal of the Left*, and we find him advancing much the same thesis as his P.O.U.M. comrades in the civil war. We must "transform the social and economic system from top to bottom," he says; and "England can only win the war by passing through revolution." A revolutionary England, he thinks, will inspire Hitler's victims in continental Europe to rebel, but "does anyone suppose that the conquered populations are going to rebel on behalf of the British dividend drawers?" He uses similar arguments in his patriotic essay

The Lion and the Unicorn. But even in his most enthusiastic flights he is realistic enough to remember
that a democratic socialist revolution requires the support of a large part of the middle class. He hopes that
naval officers, for example, would support a socialist
revolution if they could be made to see "that a victory
over Hitler demands the destruction of Capitalism."
This is somewhat optimistic, and also vaguely worded,
and it must be admitted that Orwell's political propagandist writing in the narrow sense of the word "political" was often rather loose and sometimes over-
optimistic. But his unrealism was as nothing to that
of the typical left-wing intellectual. Orwell understood, what many socialists and all communists tried
to avoid seeing, that the common man, whether middle or working class, is a patriot.

Criticizing H. G. Wells for having underrated the
power of Germany, he wrote in 1941:

> The energy that actually shapes the world springs from
> emotions—racial pride, leader worship, religious belief,
> love of war—which liberal intellectuals mechanically
> write off as anachronisms, and which they have usually
> destroyed so completely in themselves as to have lost
> all power of action.
>
> The people who say that Hitler is Antichrist, or alter-
> natively the Holy Ghost, are nearer to an understand-
> ing of the truth than the intellectuals who for ten
> dreadful years have kept it up that he is merely a
> figure out of comic opera, not worth taking seriously.
> All that this idea really reflects is the sheltered condi-
> tions of English life. The Left Book Club was at bot-
> tom a product of Scotland Yard, just as the Peace
> Pledge Union is a product of the Navy."—"Wells, Hit-
> ler and the World State"

But the sheltered conditions of English life not only
made H. G. Wells incapable of understanding that
Hitler was dangerous, they also enabled many of the

pink intelligentsia to idealize Stalin and indulge in childish fantasies of violence. Having breathed in Spain a poisonous lungful of the new totalitarian air of Europe, it shocked Orwell to find on returning to safe and sheltered England that those same intellectuals who had "lost all power of action" were flaunting the up-to-date totalitarian fashions—writing poems about "necessary murder," justifying the Russian purges and, in general, as he put it, playing with fire though not even aware that fire is hot.

It was this kind of realism about fundamentals, based upon personal experience, that was Orwell's best contribution to politics.

> I have no particular love for the idealized "worker" as he appears in the bourgeois Communist's mind, but when I see an actual flesh-and-blood worker in conflict with his natural enemy, the policeman, I do not have to ask myself which side I am on.—Homage to Catalonia

His own record in Spain gave him a perfect right to speak in this rather exalted tone, but when it came to estimating the immediate, short-term interests of the "actual flesh-and-blood worker," he was apt to be sketchy and unpractical.

THERE ARE two clearly distinguishable moods in his writing after his return from Spain in 1937. One of them is blithe and sometimes even optimistic, the other is pessimistic and increasingly grim. The latter mood was no doubt influenced by his experiences under the Communist political terror in Barcelona, and it reached its fullest expression in 1984. In the former mood he wrote his essays on boys' weeklies, comic post-cards, and Dickens and the novel Coming up for Air. All these appeared in 1939, and I think their peculiar buoyancy and vigor is due to the stimulus he

received from the comradeship and idealism of the
P.O.U.M. militiamen.

> When you have had a glimpse of such a disaster as this
> —and however it ends the Spanish war will turn out
> to have been an appalling disaster, quite apart from
> the slaughter and physical suffering—the result is not
> necessarily disillusionment and cynicism. Curiously
> enough the whole experience has left me with not less
> but more belief in the decency of human beings.

This passage comes on the last page but one of *Homage to Catalonia* and it appears to me to be linked
with the passage I have already referred to, the first
words of the book:

> In the Lenin Barracks in Barcelona, the day before I
> joined the militia, I saw an Italian militiaman standing
> in front of the officers' table. . . . It was as though his
> spirit and mine had momentarily succeeded in bridging
> the gulf of language and tradition and meeting in
> utter intimacy.

This is the first occasion in any of Orwell's books
on which one feels that he really looked at, saw, and
paid attention to another human being. By paying attention I mean becoming aware of a man's *essence*
instead of merely observing him from the outside as a
bundle of characteristics and humors. And it may be
significant that this experience happened to him after
he had abandoned, or at least hazarded, his literary
career for an active combatant role in politics. To be a
war correspondent in Spain was already to hazard his
novelist's career, but now he had given up writing altogether and become a soldier. I am not, of course,
suggesting that it was a special deficiency of Orwell's
that he had hitherto never really looked at another
human being, or at least had shown no evidence of it

in his books. (The ability of a writer to identify himself with more than one character when writing a
novel, in which he was also weak, is a different and
much more superficial and quite common gift.) The
fact is that, with very rare exceptions, there is no more
evidence of the capacity for paying attention to another human being in the rest of modern literature
than there is in Orwell's work up to this date. As exceptions, I can think of D. H. Lawrence, in whom
there is abundant evidence of it, and, among living
writers, there is at least a hint of it in J. D. Salinger.
But there are not many others.

In case it should seem that I exaggerate the significance of this particular incident, here is what Orwell
himself said about it seven years later in his essay,
"Looking Back on the Spanish War":

> I never think of the Spanish war without two memories
> coming into my mind. One is of the hospital ward at
> Lerida and the rather sad voices of the wounded mili-
> tiamen singing some song with a refrain that ended—
>
> > *Una resolucion,*
> > *Luchar hast' el fin!*
>
> . . . The other memory is of the Italian militiaman
> who shook my hand in the guardroom the day I joined
> the militia. . . . When I remember—oh, how vividly!
> —his shabby uniform and fierce, pathetic, innocent face,
> the complex side-issues of the war seem to fade away
> and I see clearly that there was at any rate no doubt
> as to who was in the right. In spite of power politics
> and journalistic lying, the central issue of the war was
> the attempt of people like this to win the decent life
> which they knew to be their birthright. It is difficult to
> think of this particular man's probable end without sev-
> eral kinds of bitterness. Since I met him in the Lenin
> Barracks he was probably a Trotskyist or an Anarchist,

and in the peculiar conditions of our time, when people of that sort are not killed by the Gestapo they are usually killed by the G.P.U. But that does not affect the long-term issues. This man's face, which I saw only for a minute or two, remains with me as a sort of visual reminder of what the war was really about. He symbolises for me the flower of the European working class, harried by the police of all countries, the people who fill the mass graves of the Spanish battlefields and are now, to the tune of several millions, rotting in forced-labour camps. . . .

I never saw the Italian militiaman again, nor did I ever learn his name. It can be taken as quite certain that he is dead. Nearly two years later, when the war was visibly lost, I wrote these verses in his memory:

> *The Italian soldier shook my hand*
> *Beside the guard-room table;*
> *The strong hand and the subtle hand*
> *Whose palms are only able*
>
> *To meet within the sound of guns,*
> *But oh! what peace I knew then*
> *In gazing on his battered face*
> *Purer than any woman's!*
>
> *For the flyblown words that make me spew*
> *Still in his ears were holy,*
> *And he was born knowing what I had learned*
> *Out of books and slowly.*
>
> *The treacherous guns had told their tale*
> *And we both had bought it,*
> *But my gold brick was made of gold—*
> *Oh! who ever would have thought it?*
>
> *Good luck go with you, Italian soldier!*
> *But luck is not for the brave;*
> *What would the world give back to you?*
> *Always less than you gave.*

> *Between the shadow and the ghost,*
> *Between the white and the red,*
> *Between the bullet and the lie,*
> *Where would you hide your head?*
>
> *For where is Manuel Gonzales,*
> *And where is Pedro Aguilar,*
> *And where is Ramon Fenellosa?*
> *The earthworms know where they are.*
>
> *Your name and your deeds were forgotten*
> *Before your bones were dry,*
> *And the lie that slew you is buried*
> *Under a deeper lie;*
>
> *But the thing that I saw in your face*
> *No power can disinherit;*
> *No bomb that ever burst*
> *Shatters the crystal spirit.*

Without making any claim for Orwell as a poet, I would nevertheless assert that this poem is of central importance in his work, and that, from the psychological point of view as distinct from the literary, it might even be regarded as the pinnacle of his achievement. It is associated in my mind with a passage from Traherne:

> Every one provideth objects, but few prepare senses whereby, and light wherein, to see them. Since therefore we are born to be a burning and shining light, and whatever men learn of others, they see in the light of others' souls: I will in the light of my soul show you the Universe. Perhaps it is celestial, and will teach you how beneficial we may be to each other. I am sure it is a sweet and curious light to me: which had I wanted I would have given all the gold and silver in all worlds to have purchased. But it was the Gift of God and could not be bought with money.—*Centuries*, III, 6

6 A BREATH OF AIR

> *I dreamed I dwelt in marble halls,*
> *And woke to find it true;*
> *I wasn't born for an age like this;*
> *Was Smith? Was Jones? Were you?*
> —From "A Happy Vicar I Might Have Been"

IT MUST HAVE BEEN in 1938 that Orwell wrote:

> *No bomb that ever burst*
> *Shatters the crystal spirit.*

When he published the poem in 1943 he was not only older but sadder and in worse health. On his return from Spain the premonitions of lung trouble had become more definite and an anonymous admirer—in fact the novelist L. H. Myers—had provided money for a holiday in North Africa, on the eve of the second world war. Orwell once attributed his constitutional weakness to his having been frequently compelled to play football when he had a cold, at his preparatory school. But in any case he had driven himself so hard all his life, and especially while living as a tramp and as a militiaman, that a breakdown of health at the age of thirty-five was not surprising.

Nevertheless, it was during the years 1938–42 that he produced some of his best and certainly his most light-hearted work. It was at this time that he began writing for *Horizon*, the second of the four literary reviews with which his name was prominently associated. *The Adelphi* had helped him to get a start; *Horizon*, by publishing, among other essays by him, "The Art of Donald McGill" and "Boys' Weeklies," helped to establish him among the best-known essayists of the day; *Partisan Review* made him known in America, through his Letters from London during the war, as a leading spokesman of the English Left intellectuals; and, after the war, the brilliant but short-lived *Polemic* was to publish several of his later and more sombre politico-literary essays on the degradation of language, the interaction of politics and literature, and the prospects of literature under totalitarianism.

The essays on boys' weeklies and on the comic-postcard artist, Donald McGill, to which we have already referred several times, were brilliant examples of his originality. Poking around in little tobacconist or stationery shops in the shabby quarters of a town, Orwell observed with pleased interest many things which the average intellectual simply fails to see at all. What is it, for example, that the mysterious "masses" really read and look at and enjoy? He found out, and examined it for himself with a sympathy and zest which reveal it in an almost enchanting light. He was also quite an authority on wall and pavement chalking. In Spain during the terror that accompanied the suppression of the P.O.U.M. he had written "Visca POUM!" on walls and in restaurant cloak-rooms; and in his English war notebooks, published in *World Review* (June, 1950), he comments on the fatuousness of a slogan he saw chalked on a wall in south London by some Blackshirt or Communist (this was while Stalin and Hitler were still friends): "Cheese, not Churchill." Somebody might conceivably be prepared to die for Churchill, he points out, but who would die for cheese? In a similar spirit, he took the trouble to count and classify press advertisements and the relative wordage of news items. In the week of the fall of Tobruk, with 20,000 prisoners, he counted the number of lines devoted to this disaster in *The New Statesman* (2) and compared it with the number devoted to the temporary suppression of *The Daily Worker* (108).

DICKENS, on whom Orwell wrote, in 1939, one of his longest essays, was obviously a congenial subject, and the essay, although not strikingly original or profound, is one of his most attractive studies. He had a number of qualities in common with Dickens, some of them obvious, such as the hatred of oppression and bullying, the delighted interest in the details of the lives of ordinary people, and the championship of the conventional virtues. But they also had in common the rare gift of *disinterested* partisanship—shrewdly perceived and defined by G. K. Chesterton in his book on Dickens as a "secret moderation." In Simone Weil's language, they "knew where the balance lay" and were ready to change sides, like Justice. Unlike most crusaders, they were always aware of the danger of hypocrisy and cant and of exceeding the limits of common sense. They both grew more pessimistic about the future as they grew older, though in Orwell's case a considerable degree of pessimism was chronic, and it was only during the brief period which we are now considering that it perceptibly lightened.

Orwell concludes his essay with a description of his own mental picture of Dickens:

> . . . a man who is always fighting against something, but who fights in the open and is not frightened, the face of a man who is *generously* angry—in other words, of a nineteenth century liberal, a free intelligence, a

type hated with equal hatred by all the smelly little orthodoxies which are now contending for our souls.

This description has a defiant but optimistic ring. Had he written it a few years later, when his health and spirits were lower, there would have been a different nuance. It would have been the desperate tone of a man fighting in a last ditch.

Dickens, as Orwell observes, was not interested in psychological subtleties. But, in terms of the distinction put forward in the last chapter between the gift of identifying oneself with someone else's personality and the gift of seeing and paying attention to another person's essence, Dickens was richly endowed with the second and far greater and rarer gift—which is one of the reasons why he is a very great writer. Compared to Thackeray, however, he *was* lacking in subtlety, and Orwell's comparison between the two is extremely just. He points out that Dickens, in describing the "gentleman" class, was quite incapable of creating even such relatively subtle characters as Major Pendennis or Rawdon Crawley. Major Pendennis is a shallow old snob and Rawdon Crawley is "a thick-headed ruffian who sees nothing wrong in living for years by swindling tradesmen," yet Thackeray is able to see that according to their tortuous code neither of them are bad men:

> Major Pendennis would not sign a dud cheque, for instance. Rawdon certainly would, but on the other hand he would not desert a friend in a tight corner. Both of them would behave well on the field of battle—a thing that would not particularly appeal to Dickens. The result is that at the end one is left with a kind of amused tolerance for Major Pendennis and with something approaching respect for Rawdon. . . . Dickens would be quite incapable of this. In his hands both Rawdon and the Major would dwindle to traditional caricatures.

The fact that both the Major and Rawdon would behave well on the field of battle certainly did appeal to Orwell. Nevertheless, he connects Dickens' failure to appreciate this virtue with one of his points of superiority to Thackeray—namely, his "lack of vulgar nationalism" and his freedom from the characteristic British nineteenth-century contempt for foreigners.

Orwell's main criticism of Dickens is really a criticism of the entire Victorian age, though it is in fact doubtfully applicable to Dickens himself in his later books. It is that his ideal life, as exemplified in his "happy endings," was a sort of cosy, incestuous idleness: "a hundred thousand pounds, a quaint old house with plenty of ivy on it, a sweetly womanly wife, a horde of children, and no work." An utterly soft, sheltered life and yet, as he says, Dickens manages to make it appear desirable and happy. "No modern man could combine so much purposelessness with so much vitality." That is extremely well said, and tolerantly expressed, for Orwell might have been expected to be more severe upon Dickens' apparent failure to see anything immoral in living parasitically upon inherited wealth. But the truth is, and it is the chief weakness of Orwell's account of Dickens that he ignores it, that there are many signs in Dickens' books and in his letters that as he grew older he became more aware of this problem. *Great Expectations*, indeed, might be regarded as a sermon on the theme that the expectation of inheriting money is disastrous to a man's character.

ORWELL'S major production in 1939 was the novel *Coming up for Air*, and it is outstanding among his books in several ways. To begin with, it is scarcely at all autobiographical, which all his previous books were to some degree. Its theme is the same as that

of nearly all his writing from 1939 onwards. It foretells—what required no great gift of prophecy—the
outbreak of the second world war; but beyond that it
also foretells a new iron age of totalitarianism, with
rubber truncheons, colored shirts, food queues, slo-
gans, and sadism. It is told in the first person by
George Bowling, a fat, cheerful, red-faced insurance
man with a nagging but genteel wife and a couple of
children. More or less the comic-postcard husband, in
fact, and very unlike Orwell himself. Yet Orwell succeeds in a remarkable way, for once, in identifying
himself with this narrator and at the same time in
making him a plausible mouthpiece for his own opinions. George Bowling is a completely different character from the angry young man of *Keep the Aspidistra Flying* or the weary middle-aged protagonist of
1984. He is a thoroughly commonplace common man,
yet he is not only decent and kind; he is also extremely intelligent, though not at all intellectual. To
have created such a convincing and agreeable symbol
of the fundamental goodness and sanity of the common man is a considerable achievement.

Most of George Bowling's instincts are conservative
and the plot of the novel is concerned with his disillusionment when he returns to the country town where
he was brought up and finds that it has been enlarged,
industrialized and modernized beyond recognition. He
is not a simpleton, however. He sees clearly that people
like himself, small employees of big corporations, are
in the same boat as the industrial working classes and
are getting an equally shabby deal. Nevertheless, one
cannot imagine him on the barricades and it is probable that if he survived the blitz of 1940 he would
have greeted his creator's exhortations in 1941 to
"transform the social and economic system from top
to bottom" with a skeptical and not too discreet rasp-

berry. He does, however, represent the great mass of ordinary decent people who, according to the argument of *The Road to Wigan Pier*, could be converted to socialism if only socialists were not such a bad advertisement for their own faith, so priggish, so dictatorial and so freakish.

By a lucky chance, he finds himself in possession of a small sum of money, enough for a few days' holiday, which his wife does not yet know he has got; and instead of spending it on a bout of infidelity he decides to revisit his childhood home, telling his wife that he is on a business trip to Birmingham. All he really wants is a little peace, and to immerse himself in the golden memories of his pre-1914 childhood. As he turns off the Birmingham road toward his home town of Lower Binfield, he has such a guilty feeling that he peeps through the car's rear window to see if *they* are following him.

> When I say *they* I mean all the people who wouldn't approve of a trip of this kind and who'd have stopped me if they could—which, I suppose, would include pretty well everybody.

He imagines a huge army racing along the road after him, led by his wife "with the kids tagging after her," the neighbors, his employers in their Rolls Royces and Hispano Suizas, all the other clerks who live in his suburb, with their families, and finally:

> . . . all the soul-savers and Nosey Parkers, the people whom you've never seen but who rule your destiny just the same, the Home Secretary, Scotland Yard, the Temperance League, the Bank of England, Lord Beaverbrook, Hitler and Stalin on a tandem bicycle, the bench of Bishops, Mussolini, the Pope—they were all of them after me. I could almost hear them shouting: "There's a chap who thinks he's going to escape! There's a chap

who says he won't be streamlined! He's going back to Lower Binfield! After him! Stop him!"

He doesn't want to be streamlined. It is really the same situation as Gordon Comstock's and Winston Smith's, but transposed into the key of comedy.

Poor Bowling has married, definitely above his class, the daughter of a retired Anglo-Indian official. She is a virtuous but depressing wife, because her spirit was broken long before she met him by the typical Anglo-Indian struggle to maintain genteel standards on an insufficient income. (This feature of the book seems to reflect Orwell's view of his own family.) As George Bowling puts it, "the idea of doing things because you enjoy them is something she can hardly understand"; and he perceives that there is more awareness and *feeling* of poverty in impoverished upper-class families than in many really poor families of the working class. Even after he gets a salary rise Hilda, his wife, continues her cheese-paring as remorselessly as before, buying a breakfast marmalade with a label announcing in small print that it contains "a certain proportion of neutral fruit juice." This sets him meditating—unfortunately, aloud—upon mock turtles grazing in a grove of neutral fruit trees. But in spite of the nagging and bickering it is not an altogether bad or unhappy family life, though one has no difficulty in understanding his need of a short rest.

What he gets, however, is a series of shocks and disillusionments as he finds that the country town of his golden memories has become almost indistinguishable from the London suburb where he now lives. He returns home in the knowledge that the old stable individualistic world which he remembers is gone for ever. The climax of his disillusionment is his discovery that his secret fishing pool in the woods has been drained and turned into a rubbish dump by a colony of Simple Lifers who have cut down all the trees to make room for their Garden City, leaving one clump around the desecrated pool, which they call the Pixy Glen.

Apart from these—inevitably, sandaled—Simple Lifers, the only "progressive" character in the book is a lecturer who is introduced by his chairman as Mr. So-and-so, "the well-known anti-Fascist." Bowling's comment:

> A queer trade, anti-Fascism. This fellow, I suppose, makes his living by writing books against Hitler. But what did he do before Hitler came along? And what'll he do if Hitler ever disappears?

He concludes that the lecturer's real business in life is simply *Hate*.

> Hitler's after us! Quick! Let's all grab a spanner and get together, and perhaps if we smash in enough faces they won't smash ours. Gang up, choose your Leader. Hitler's black, and Stalin's white. But it might just as well be the other way about because in the little chap's mind both Hitler and Stalin are the same. Both mean spanners and smashed faces.

Finally he realizes that that is what the future is going to be. There will always be faces to be smashed by spanners and little men like the anti-Fascist lecturer will always have a job inciting people to smash them. From this to the grim vision of Big Brother in 1984 is a simple and straightforward development. But *Coming up for Air* is a totally different sort of book. In spite of the depressing message its spirit is hopeful and humorous.

The reason would appear to be that when he wrote it Orwell was still influenced by the memory of the warmth and hospitality he met with in the homes of the unemployed in Lancashire and Yorkshire and by

the comradeship and heroism of the civil war militiamen. But the five long years of the world war, and his
illness, and his wife's death in 1945, seem to have
quenched his always rather precarious optimism. In
his two postwar novels, *Animal Farm* and *1984*,
neither the common man, as in *Coming up for Air*,
nor the working class is conceived as having any power
to counteract the decadence of the intellectuals and
the bestiality of the hatemongering political fanatics.
The "crystal spirit" may not have been shattered, but
it is in a dark and total eclipse. Writing, in 1946, of
the failure of intellectuals to defend intellectual liberty,
he was to say that "the big public do not care about
the matter one way or the other. They are not in favour
of persecuting the heretic, and they will not exert
themselves to defend him. They are at once too sane
and too stupid to acquire the totalitarian outlook. The
direct, conscious attack on intellectual decency comes
from the intellectuals themselves." ("The Prevention
of Literature.") But in 1939 George Bowling was not
stupid.

THE TEMPTATION must be resisted of picturing Orwell's development in a neat graph as a curve that
ascends from *Down and Out in Paris and London* to
Coming up for Air and then descends to *1984*. That
there was a striking change of mood in 1936, when he
became an active socialist, is obvious; and it is possible
to suggest reasons for it. After years of fighting a lone
battle against hostile society and the indifferent stars
he suddenly saw that there was a *social* struggle in
progress. He felt a sense of community with the unemployed in the north of England and the militiamen
in Spain, and he saw there was a place for him by
their side. But the change of mood between *Coming
up for Air* and *1984* is much subtler and less abrupt

and it would be rash to assign causes or even to attempt a clear-cut definition of it. Does *Animal Farm* prove that he believed that revolutions would always be betrayed? Does *1984* prove that he believed the human spirit would inevitably founder in a soulless mechanical totalitarianism? Obviously, it was just because he believed the issues were still undecided that he thought it worth while to write these terrible warnings.

On the personal level, there is no doubt that up to the end he believed, or hoped, that his lungs would mend; and he died with his head full of plans for future books. He hoped to write novels of a different kind. Could he have done so? We shall never know. But there are indications in *Coming up for Air* and elsewhere that he was capable of a more contemplative and psychological approach. He manages to make it appear plausible that the fat cheerful George Bowling should understand the impulse of a hermit to retire to the desert.

> But it wasn't that I wanted to watch my navel. I only wanted to get my nerve back before the bad times begin. . . . Perhaps a war, perhaps a slump—there's no knowing, except that it'll be something bad. . . . And you can't face that kind of thing unless you've got the right feeling inside you. There's something that's gone out of us in these twenty years since the war. It's a kind of vital juice that we've squirted away until there is nothing left.

And in some of the charming pieces of weekly journalism which he wrote for *Tribune* after 1945 there is poetic imagination and subtle responsiveness to atmosphere, as for example in his evocation of nineteenth-century New England in "Riding Down From Bangor" (included in *Shooting an Elephant*). And there is something touching in his patient replies to

correspondents who accuse him of bourgeois sentimentality and escapism every time he mentions a
flower or a bird. This type of correspondent thinks
that a socialist journalist should never write about
anything except what is unpleasant, so as to keep
discontent and militancy on the boil.

> Certainly, Orwell replies, we ought to be discontented.
> We ought not simply to find out ways of making the
> best of a bad job and yet if we kill all pleasure in the
> actual process of life, what sort of future are we prepar-
> ing for ourselves? If a man cannot enjoy the return of
> Spring, why should he be happy in a labour-saving
> Utopia? . . . I have always suspected that if our eco-
> nomic and political problems are ever solved life will
> become simpler instead of more complex, and that the
> sort of pleasure one gets from finding the first primrose
> will loom larger than the sort of pleasure one gets from
> eating an ice to the tune of a Wurlitzer.

They are at once too sane and too stupid . . .
  —From "The Prevention of Literature"

IN 1947 ORWELL wrote a long essay on *The English People* for a series entitled "Britain in Pictures." It begins with some shrewd and affectionate touches characterizing the gentleness, decency, artistic insensibility and parochialism of the English. One of our most remarkable habits, he says, in contrast with most modern countries, is that of "not killing one another." But we are obstinate, and we willingly accept for our national emblem the bulldog, "an animal noted for its obstinacy, ugliness and impenetrable stupidity." The remainder of the essay, however, is a rather tired and colorless repetition of the war-time essay, *The Lion and the Unicorn*. In the latter he had been impatient for the drastic, though vaguely conceived, transformation of a society in which "common soldiers risk their lives for two-and-sixpence a day, and fat women ride about in Rolls-Royce cars, nursing Pekingeses." But in *The English People* he is politically much milder and seems, indeed, to assume that reforms in the direction of social and economic equality had progressed further than was in fact the case.

Some time between 1941 and 1947 the main burden of his political animosity seems to have subtly shifted. In "Inside the Whale" (1940) the unpatriotic, deracinated intellectual was one of his principal *bêtes noires*. The "Communism" of the English intellectual, he said, was simply the patriotism of the deracinated. The other big *bête noire* was, of course, the capitalist boss. But already by 1943, in "Poetry and the Microphone," the bureaucrat with his "genteel throaty voice" begins to subsume in his own person both the boss and the delinquent intellectual. This proves, I think, that Orwell was both prescient and realistic. He worked in broadcasting during the war, and he was already beginning to see where the real danger lay—the enormous power of a technological bureaucracy.

But what is pathetic and, one hopes, less realistic in both *Animal Farm* (which appeared in 1945) and 1984, is the helpless, inert, and almost imbecile role which he attributes to the common man. In Spain and in his books from 1936 to 1939 the common man had been his hero; and he himself had come to be regarded as the common man's particular champion, interpreter and spokesman. But in *Animal Farm* the common man becomes a good-hearted, dim-witted cart horse who works himself to death for a gang of pigs. This is of course not a hostile portrait or an unkind one. But it is terribly pessimistic, and it will be worth while to look at what Orwell says about the genesis of the idea of *Animal Farm*, in the preface to the Ukrainian edition. He begins by referring to his experience in Barcelona during the purge of the Trotskyists, when many of his P.O.U.M. friends were shot, and others were in prison for a long time or simply disappeared. This purge, he points out, was like a minor supplement to the great purges going on in Russia at the same time. He then describes his astonishment, when he returned to England, on finding that sensible and normally well-informed people were believing both what they read in the left-wing press about the treachery of the P.O.U.M., which he knew to be false, and also the similar stories about the guilt of the innumerable accused in the Russian mass-purges. This convinced him that the myth of the justice and infallibility of the Soviet régime must be exploded before there could be any effective revival of the socialist movement in Europe. The problem was to denounce the Soviet myth in a simple story which almost any reader could understand and which could be easily translated into other languages. He took a long time to think it over. It was six years before he actually wrote the story, and another two before it was published, in 1945.

The basic idea for the story occurred to him one day in the country when he saw a little boy of about ten years old driving a huge horse along a narrow lane, whipping it whenever it tried to turn aside. "It struck me that if only such animals became conscious of their strength we should have no power over them; and that ordinary people exploit animals in much the same way as the rich exploit the proletariat."

A simple idea, which he developed into a short book of not much more than 30,000 words. But it placed him among the most famous writers of his day. He had envisaged the possibility of translations, but perhaps he hardly foresaw that it was going to be printed in almost every script in the world, including Japanese, Persian and Russian, or that at least one of its sentences was going to become a household word throughout Western civilization: "All animals are equal but some animals are more equal than others." The idea of the Seven Commandments which were mysteriously modified from time to time—"No animal shall drink alcohol" becoming "No animal shall drink alcohol to excess"; "All animals are equal" becoming "All animals are equal but," etc.—was borrowed, of course, from Swift. In form and style the book is obviously a little masterpiece; but it is based upon an analogy which has awkward implications.

INSPIRED by a prophetic dream of Old Major, a prize Middle White boar, the animals of the Manor Farm drive out their bad farmer, Mr. Jones, and set up an Animals' Republic. The farm is renamed Animal Farm and the book relates its fortunes up to the day when the original name is restored and "friendly" relations are re-established with the neighboring human farmers. The struggle of the farm animals, having driven out their human exploiter, to create a free and equal community takes the form of a most ingeniously worked-out recapitulation of the history of Soviet Russia from 1917 up to the Teheran Conference, which is symbolized by a game of cards between the pig-dictator Napoleon and a human neighbor, Mr. Pilkington. Suddenly each of them plays an ace of spades simultaneously, and the frightened farm animals, watching from outside the parlor window the violent quarrel which ensues, are unable any longer to distinguish the pig's face from the man's.

The moral, of course, is that the animals' revolution has been betrayed by the selfishness and will to power of the pigs who, like the Communist Party in Russia, have controlled it from the beginning; and that the living conditions of the animals are in the end no better than they were under their human exploiters. In developing this theme Orwell discovered in himself a new vein of fantasy, humor and tenderness. His love of animals and of country life, his mastery of a clear, terse and flowing prose style, and the passionate purpose behind his use of it combined to produce an almost magical effect, and the story was read with absorption not only by the grownups for whom it was intended but also by children who had not the slightest inkling of its political moral.

Animal Farm is so well known that it cannot be necessary to do more than mention some of its major felicities: the friendship between the noble, dim-witted cart horse Boxer and the resigned, cynical and clear-headed donkey Benjamin; the incorrigible behavior of Mollie, the white mare who used to draw Mr. Jones' trap (when the animals first explore the farmhouse she is discovered admiring herself in a mirror "in a very foolish manner," and later she deserts to the enemy, having been lured away, by a man, with presents of sugar and red ribbon); and the perfidy of Napoleon, who sells Boxer to a Slaughterer and Glue Boiler when his strength has given out after years of Herculean labor for the farm.

The immediate, terrific impact of *Animal Farm* was perhaps partly due to the fact that the high tide of Russian popularity in England after Stalingrad was already ebbing in 1945, when the book was published. But it had in fact been almost completed by 1943, when Orwell was one of the very few whose experience and knowledge prevented them from indulging in rosy hopes of future sympathy and understanding between Russia and the West.

The air of blitheness and buoyancy which fills *Animal Farm*, as it does *Homage to Catalonia*, in spite of the depressing theme, suggests that Orwell was still comparatively optimistic when he wrote it. But by comparing the working class to animals, even noble and attractive ones, he implies that they are at an irremediable disadvantage in the class struggle. The animals' difficulty in using tools is emphasized several times in the book; and it is only the clever but repulsive and odious pigs who are able to learn to use a pen, walk on two legs, and pass themselves off as human beings. One is reminded of Orwell's attitude many years earlier, when he returned from Burma at the age of twenty-four:

> At that time failure seemed to me the only virtue. Every suspicion of self-advancement, even to "succeed" in life to the extent of earning a few hundreds a year, seemed to me spiritually ugly, a species of bullying.

It will be remembered that *Keep the Aspidistra Flying* was about a young man who held a sort of immature and self-centered version of the above doctrine; and although Orwell himself, having once found a political purpose for his writing, never relapsed into the mood of that early novel, it does appear in *Animal Farm*, and still more in 1984, that he ceased to rely upon the generous, humane and unambitious instincts—the "crystal spirit"—of the common man as an effective political ally in the struggle against spiritual ugliness and bullying. And from a certain point of view 1984 can be seen as a restatement of the theme of *Keep the Aspidistra Flying* on a more comprehensive scale and with a deeper political and social and philosophical awareness.

NOW THAT we have looked at Orwell's work and sketched his career up to the pinnacle of success, when he had only five more years to live, this may be a suitable place to say a word about the man himself. Even during the embittered years when he was writing his first three novels he always seemed to be on the surface the easiest and most affable of men. Pleasant, humorous, witty, considerate, gentle; but unpredictable. Below the surface it was conceivable that he might be "awkward." Actually, below the surface he was extremely reserved and undemonstrative—exceptionally endowed with *pudor*. His wife died suddenly and unexpectedly, under an anaesthetic for a minor operation, in 1945; and I suspect that this was a far more grievous blow than he allowed it to appear. Materially, it certainly made life much more difficult for a middle-aged man with an adopted baby and precarious health. He was to be married once more, but not until 1949, when he had only a few months to live. His second wife, Sonia Brownell, another charming and brilliant woman, had a footing of her own in the literary circles of both London and Paris.

In the meantime, immediately after the war, he had rented a disused farmhouse on a remote island of the Inner Hebrides, where he at first intended to spend only the summer months. But he soon began to spend all his time there, except for periods in sanatoria on the mainland. He was writing 1984 and, at such times as he was well enough to be up and about, living a rough and hard life extremely unsuited to the state of his health. During this period his unmarried sister, Avril Blair, took care of him and the baby and ran the house singlehanded—an achievement which can only be appreciated by those who have lived on a Hebridean island in a house separated from the single general store by twenty-five miles of almost impracticable road. They lived on the undemonstrative terms that seem to have been normal among members of their family. On one occasion when I was there I remember Orwell returning from the mainland after a very stormy crossing. What had chiefly impressed him was the terrible plight of one of the women passengers. She had been so ill as to seem to be dying. Orwell had been sick too, but he insisted on the impression this poor woman had made on him: "She had completely collapsed; and it made me think how terrible it must be to be a woman, so weak and easily upset . . ." His sister, who had never been seasick in her life, made no comment.

Orwell never really lost a certain boyish, Robinson Crusoe spirit, and dangers and hardships had a sort of tempting fascination for him. The sea around the island was particularly dangerous, with tideraces and eddies; and there was one famous whirlpool which at certain states of the tide was capable of engulfing a small steamship. Orwell took risks with it and finally wrecked his small boat, losing the outboard engine, and getting marooned on a providential rock with his three-and-a-half-year-old boy. These were the sort of conditions, entirely unsuitable for a middle-aged consumptive, in which he wrote his last and most famous novel.

1984 IS NOT so obviously a masterpiece as *Animal Farm*; but it is wider and more ambitious in scope and has probably been even more influential. It, too, contains images and phrases—Big Brother, for example, and *doublethink*—which have become familiar throughout Western civilization; and it is perhaps mainly thanks to this book that the adjective "Orwellian" can be used wherever English is spoken with almost the same probability of being understood as "Shavian" or "Wellsian." Yet it is not easy to decide how good a book it really is. Writing of *Uncle Tom's Cabin* Orwell called it the supreme example of what he thought of as "good bad" books. "It is an unintentionally ludicrous book, full of preposterous melodramatic incidents; it is also deeply moving and essentially true." ("Good Bad Books" in *Shooting an Elephant*.) He further prophesied that it would outlast the entire works of George Moore and Virginia Woolf, although he could think of no strictly literary test by which its superiority could be proved.

Without conceding that it need be called in any way a bad book, I would make the same prophecy about *1984*, and I would add the entire works of Joyce, with the doubtful exception of *Ulysses*, to the list of shorter-lived books. *1984* is full of melodramatic incidents, but they are not preposterous in the sense of being artistically inappropriate or even—fantastic though one hopes this will some day appear—particularly hard to believe. They are, however, in one or two places rather flatly written and one of them might be called unintentionally ludicrous. But although Orwell must often have been feeling tired and ill when he was writing the book, it has very few weak passages and is, in the main, a sustained and powerful imaginative effort which very few contemporary novelists could approach.

Among Orwell's earlier heroes Gordon Comstock was in rebellion against the money god who commanded him to become a conventional business man; and George Bowling, more modestly, wanted merely to avoid being streamlined, and to be able to call his soul his own, though he lived in fear of a coming regime of thugs with rubber truncheons. But in *1984* Winston Smith is already living under a regime far worse than any that Gordon could have imagined and in which George's worst fears have been realized.

> It was a bright cold day in April, and the clocks were striking thirteen. Winston Smith, his chin nuzzled into his breast in an effort to escape the vile wind, slipped quickly through the glass doors of Victory Mansions, though not quickly enough to prevent a swirl of gritty dust from entering along with him.

That is the first paragraph of *1984*. Except for the twenty-four-hour clock it recalls the first paragraph of *Coming up for Air*:

> The idea really came to me the day I got my new false teeth. I remember the morning well. At about a quarter

to eight I'd nipped out of bed and got into the bath-
room just in time to shut the kids out. It was a beastly
January morning, with a dirty yellowish-grey sky. . . .

And of *The Clergyman's Daughter:*

As the alarm clock on the chest of drawers exploded
like a horrid little bomb of bell metal, Dorothy,
wrenched from the depths of some complex, troubling
dream, awoke with a start and lay on her back looking
into the darkness with extreme exhaustion.

Poor Winston is going to share Dorothy's extreme exhaustion and not George Bowling's cheerfulness and
vigor.

He was born in 1945 and has lived through an atomic
war and the subsequent period of social disturbances
out of which the world of the 1980's has crystallized.
There are three great world powers—Oceania, Eurasia
and Eastasia—which correspond, though only roughly,
to the actual power blocs of the present day. There is a
continuous desultory war between them which none
of them seriously desires to bring to an end, because a
state of war creates a favorable atmosphere for their
home policies. The three world empires, in fact, prop
one another up "like three sheaves of corn." Oceania
consists of the Americas, the British Commonwealth,
and the British Isles, the latter being known as Air-
strip One, with London for its capital. The social and
economic system is as follows: a ruling Party (with a,
possibly fictitious and merely symbolic, Leader known
as Big Brother) divided into two branches, the Inner
Party and the Outer Party. The Inner Party members
are the rulers and the Outer Party, to which Winston
belongs, consists of secretarial and technical employees. The remaining 85 per cent of the population are
known as "the proles"; they have no rights and no
responsibilities and are regarded as of no more po-

litical significance than animals. The economic system is nominally socialist in that all private ownership, except of petty personal possessions, has been abolished. All property belongs to the State, represented by the Inner Party.

In all this, Orwell is merely exaggerating the tendencies he observed in the world of his day; and he succeeds in packing into 1984 nearly all the ideas of all his previous books. 1984 is often compared to Aldous Huxley's *Brave New World* as though one of them will prove to be a more correct prophecy than the other. But it is their resemblances rather than their differences that are significant. Orwell and Huxley are disturbed by much the same features of twentieth-century life, and the only important difference between them is that Huxley predicts that the hypertrophy of these features will be due to a combination of sloth, or apathy, with brutish hedonism, while according to Orwell it will be due to the same sloth or apathy combined with brutish will-to-power. Why should there not be a large measure of truth in both diagnoses? The ruling Party in 1984 is an oligarchy which appears to have discovered the secret of retaining power indefinitely. It has understood that "the secret of rulership is to combine a belief in one's own infallibility with the power to learn from past mistakes." It does this by correcting its mistakes, but falsifying the past so as to prove that the mistakes were never made; and its members prove this not only to their subjects but to themselves, by the technique of *doublethink*.

> The new aristocracy was made up for the most part of bureaucrats, scientists, technicians, trade-union organisers, publicity experts, sociologists, teachers, journalists and professional politicians . . . As compared with their opposite numbers [i.e. ruling castes] in past ages,

they were less avaricious, less tempted by luxury, *hungrier for pure power* [my italics] and, above all, more conscious of what they were doing and more intent on crushing opposition . . .

For the student of Orwell the composition of the new aristocracy is very significant. Triumphant progressivism has shaken off the nudists and sandal-wearers; the "little fat men" of *The Road to Wigan Pier* have become robot bureaucrats with fruity voices and spectacles which in certain lights produce the effect of "two blank discs instead of eyes"; and the folly of the intellectuals in the nineteen-thirties has sown seeds which have blossomed into a full-blown sadism:

> . . . in the general hardening of outlook that set in round about 1930, practices which had long since been abandoned, in some cases for hundreds of years—imprisonment without trial, the use of war prisoners as slaves, public executions, torture to extract confessions, the use of hostages and the deportation of whole populations—not only became common again, but were tolerated and even defended by people who considered themselves enlightened and progressive.

That is from a heretical (but true) history of the twentieth century issued by the Party as a trap for Party members who are suspected of being recalcitrant to the official "truth." It represents, of course, a logical development of Orwell's own views as expressed in his earlier books. Of twentieth-century socialism it speaks as follows:

> . . . in each variant of Socialism that appeared from about 1900 onwards the aim of establishing liberty and equality was more and more openly abandoned. The new movements which appeared in the middle years of the century, Ingsoc in Oceania, Neo-Bolshevism in Eurasia, Death-Worship, as it is commonly called, in East-

asia, had the conscious aim of perpetuating *un*freedom
and *in*equality.

The oligarchy is adoptive and not hereditary; it re-
cruits, by examination, intelligent children from the
Outer Party. But it deals with the proles in the manner
of the Spartans with their helots. The Thought Police
take no interest in their opinions but simply liquidate
any of them who show signs of initiative or originality.
Party members, on the other hand, are spied upon con-
tinuously by microphone and "telescreen" (two-way
television) and are tortured and brain-washed if they
show the faintest sign of lapsing from orthodoxy. All
this, too, is a consistent development of Orwell's former predictions. But there are two new features in
1984 which require examination. One is his apparent
belief that the oligarchy would be able to treat the
proles (85 per cent of the population) as a negligible
factor, and the other is the theory that the oligarchy
could survive indefinitely with a philosophy, or religion, limited to pure sadistic love of power.

To take the second and simpler point first. O'Brien,
the Party philosopher who is concerned with the purg-
ing of Winston's heresy, explains the Party's philosophy as follows:

> Power is in inflicting pain and humiliation. Power is in
> tearing human minds to pieces and putting them to-
> gether again in new shapes of your own choosing. Do
> you begin to see, then, what kind of world we are creat-
> ing? It is the exact opposite of the stupid hedonistic
> Utopias that the old reformers imagined. A world of
> fear and treachery and torment, a world of trampling
> and being trampled upon, a world which will grow not
> less but *more* merciless as it refines itself. Progress in
> our world will be towards more pain . . . Always we
> shall have the heretic here at our mercy, screaming with
> pain, broken up, contemptible—and in the end utterly

penitent, saved from himself, crawling to our feet of his own accord. . . . A world of victory after victory, triumph after triumph after triumph: an endless pressing, pressing, pressing upon the nerve of power.

I do not suggest that sentiments like this are incredible. Other writers—D. H. Lawrence, for example —have shown good reason for believing that the world of atheistic science and machinery is uprooting the human psyche and thwarting its natural growth and will end by distorting it into monstrous shapes. But in Orwell's case it does appear that his actual *writing* changes for the worse when the dialogue between O'Brien and Winston begins: and in order to judge the above passage we need to retrace Winston's story up to this point.

He is an editor in the Ministry of Truth, where his job is to rewrite the past, as recorded in back numbers of newspapers, so as to make it correspond with the Party's present policy. He is a social misfit, a harborer of unorthodox thoughts, and a predestined victim of the Thought Police. He gets involved in an excruciatingly dangerous love affair with Julia, another secret rebel. He shares some of Orwell's own characteristics. For example, he is attracted by the fine, creamy quality of the paper in an old, or pre-1940, notebook which he buys in a junk shop and uses for a secret diary (his first overt step toward perdition); he is troubled by a cough in the mornings; and he has dreams of a holiday in a Golden Country in the Thames valley, where there are beech woods and slow streams with dace swimming in the pools under the willow trees. As an intellectual he resembles Gordon Comstock and in his nostalgia for the past and for a country life he resembles George Bowling; and the points in which he resembles them are the points in which they resemble their common author. He rents a room over the junk shop, where he and Julia can be together on the rare occasions when they dare snatch a few hours from their "voluntary" after-hours work for the Party. Needless to say, they have walked into a trap. The proprietor of the shop is a member of the Thought Police.

One day they are looking out of the window at a prole woman hanging out diapers on a washing line. It occurs to Winston that the proles are at least keeping the body and the instincts alive through the years of tyranny, and that if he and his kind can keep the mind alive then surely some day the proles will awaken to mental life; and although he will be dead he will at least have contributed to the life of the future.

"We are the dead," he said.
"We are the dead," echoed Julia dutifully.
"You are the dead," said an iron voice behind them.

They are about to be arrested, and the voice comes from a telescreen hidden behind a picture.

"It was behind the picture," said Julia.
"It was behind the picture," said the voice.

The picture suddenly falls.

"Now they can see us," said Julia.
"Now we can see you," said the voice.

A little later:

"The house is surrounded," said Winston.
"The house is surrounded," said the voice.
He heard Julia snap her teeth together. "I suppose we may as well say good-bye," she said.
"You may as well say good-bye," said the voice.

From then on the story becomes a catalogue of horrors, and this rather flat introduction to them, with the overworked repetitions, does suggest to me that

Orwell was tired when he reached this point in the book. After weeks, or months, in the cells of the Ministry of Love, Winston is allowed to see himself in a mirror and he breaks down in tears on seeing his ravaged face and wasted frame. It is tragically likely that the whole account of his interrogation and torture, including the exposition of the Party's sadistic philosophy—"pressing, pressing, pressing upon the nerve of power"—is a reflection of Orwell's sense of the ruthless ravages of consumption upon his own body. He survived the publication of the book by only seven months.

The first three-quarters of the book are a brilliant, macabre and convincing picture of what life might be like under a totalitarian oligarchy, but it does rather weaken the force of the warning when the dynamic of the system is described in such lurid and over-simple terms. I am convinced that Orwell would have conceived the last part of the book more subtly if his health had not been breaking down.

THE OTHER FEATURE of 1984, besides the Party philosophy, which calls for comment is the description of the proles. Although they constitute 85 per cent of the population, nobody pays any attention to them—except for the Thought Police's periodical liquidation of any outstanding personalities who might cause trouble. They are left to run wild in their slums. "Proles and animals are free." Even the older among them have only hazy memories of the first half of the century, and the constant rewriting of history and news items makes any general knowledge of the past impossible. So they have no means of knowing whether their conditions have improved or deteriorated. Winston Smith's attitude toward them varies. "If there is hope," he wrote in his diary, "it lies in the proles."

If they ever became conscious of their own strength, they would only need to rise up and shake themselves "like a horse shaking off flies." But he is very seldom able to feel any hope. "When you put it into words it sounded reasonable: it was when you looked at the human beings passing you in the street that it became an act of faith."

The real trouble seems to be that when Winston looks at the proles he sees them, as Orwell himself was once inclined to do, as comic post-card figures: "Two bloated women, one of them with her hair coming down, had got hold of the same saucepan . . ." Or an old man reminiscing in a pub: "Quite the gent, 'e was—dress shirt, top 'at, black overcoat. 'E was kind of zig-zagging across the pavement, and I bumps into 'im accidental-like. 'E says, 'Why can't you look where you're going?' 'e says. I says, 'Ju think you've bought the bleeding pavement?' "; or a street scene: "Girls in full bloom, with crudely lipsticked mouths, and youths who chased the girls, and swollen waddling women who showed you what the girls would look like in ten years' time." No wonder his idea of salvation through the proles appears to him "a mystical truth and a palpable absurdity." And in any case, as we learned from *Animal Farm,* even when the proles do arise and shake themselves like a horse shaking off flies the only result is that they fall under the domination of pigs.

Every one is familiar with the mood in which any belief in human beings in the mass is an act of faith and a palpable absurdity. Think of the rush hour in the tubes, of a bargain sale, of people reading newspapers or queuing up for the movies. It is absurd to dream of these people rising up like a giant and creating a glorious future. But the mood in which they appear capable of degenerating permanently into the demoralized mob described in 1984 is also only a mood. Yet the plausibility of the book does partly depend upon an uncritical acceptance of this mood.

An important symbol in the book is the "monstrous woman" who spends most of her day between the washtub and the clothesline outside the window of the room where Winston and Julia meet. And she is the occasion of one of the only two passages in which Winston succeeds in contemplating the proles with a little imagination. This woman of fifty is always singing, some trashy popular song, but her voice is still sweet and it suddenly strikes Winston that in her own way she is beautiful. "The solid, contourless body, like a block of granite, and the rasping red skin bore the same relation to the body of a girl as the rose-hip to the rose." And after thirty years of laundering, scrubbing, darning, cooking, sweeping, polishing, mending for children and grandchildren, there she was, still singing.

> The proles were immortal, you could not doubt it when you looked at that valiant figure in the yard. In the end their awakening would come. And until that happened, though it might be a thousand years, they would stay alive against all the odds, like birds, passing on from body to body the vitality which the Party did not share and could not kill.

This is very well; but all the same he still sees the woman as barely human. Touching and pathetic, perhaps, but "monstrous"—this adjective recurs almost every time a prole woman is mentioned. One is reminded of the "twenty scarlet faces" of the "prosperous plumbers" in *Keep the Aspidistra Flying*.

Intellectuals seem to have the greatest difficulty in seeing the unintellectual masses as human beings. Most novelists avoid the problem by not writing about them, though here again D. H. Lawrence is the outstanding exception. It is true to say that no single character in any book by Lawrence is seen as a comic post-card caricature. For him, members of all classes are human and all are equally interestingly human. Another exception, sometimes, is Orwell himself; and on one other occasion in 1984 he allows Winston Smith to meditate with some perceptiveness about the proles.

> They were not loyal to a party or a country or an idea, they were loyal to one another. *For the first time in his life* [my italics] he did not despise the proles or think of them merely as an inert force which would one day spring to life and regenerate the world. The proles had stayed human. They had not become hardened inside. They had held on to the primitive emotions which he himself had to re-learn by conscious effort.

There is an echo here, but a rather forlorn echo, of the poem which Orwell wrote, on his return from Spain, about the Italian soldier.

> . . . he was born knowing what I had learned
> Out of books and slowly.

The poem does not show the Italian soldier as a beefy garlic-stinking desperado—which from the Winston Smith point of view he probably was—but as a vehicle of the crystal spirit. Yet his mother may very well have been just such a broad-buttocked, brawny, contourless "monster" as the prole woman in 1984.

AS OPPOSED to the depressing emphasis upon the monstrousness of the prole woman, the figure of Julia is the one point of relief and contrast against the nightmarish horror of the book. Not that she would be remarkable in the work of a more subtle and sensitive novelist; but in Orwell's work she stands out as his liveliest and most perceptive study of a woman. The shallow and frigid Elizabeth of *Burmese Days* and the warm, generous Rosemary of *Keep the Aspidistra Flying* (based upon the character of his wife Eileen) are well described; but they are no more than sketches of features in the human landscape surrounding the hero. Julia is something more. If, as is probable, she can be taken as representing Orwell's idea of essential femininity, it is a somewhat "reactionary" portrait, although not really very different from the "progressive" Bernard Shaw's typical woman. Julia is intelligent but completely unintellectual, determined, practical, unscrupulous, capable of generosity but rather narrowly single-minded. Above all, she is realistic and a vigorous puncturer of hypocrisy and cant. She is brilliantly successful in deceit—"I am rather good at staying alive" is how she puts it—but prepared to take extraordinary risks to gain her ends.

The middle-aged Winston is astonished at the coarseness of her language, but is rather pleased by it. "It was merely one symptom of her revolt against the Party and all its ways, and somehow it seemed natural and healthy, like the sneeze of a horse that smells bad hay." With her tough vitality and ability to survive and even enjoy life against overwhelming odds, her self-absorption and total indifference to the wider issues of truth and justice, and her lack of interest in the past and the future, she strikes a poignant note in the book and makes a dramatic contrast to the tormented, far-seeing Winston. The essential difference between them, and Orwell probably meant it to illustrate the difference between men and women, is hinted at when they visit the enigmatic and formidable O'Brien to offer their services to the underground organization against the Party, which they believe exists; and of which they believe, or at least hope, rashly and mistakenly, that he is a leader. O'Brien asks them to what lengths they are prepared to go. Will they commit murder, treason, blackmail, forgery, disseminate venereal diseases, give their lives, and so on? They answer "Yes." Then are they prepared to separate and never see one another again?

"No!" broke in Julia.

It appeared to Winston that a long time passed before he answered. For a moment he seemed even to have been deprived of the power of speech. His tongue worked soundlessly, forming the opening syllables first of one word, then of the other, over and over again. Until he had said it, he did not know which word he was going to say. "No," he said finally.

> Under the spreading chestnut tree
> I sold you and you sold me.
>
> —From 1984

THERE IS ONE MORE FEATURE OF 1984, and perhaps
the most significant of all, that remains to be considered. It is the purpose and the effect of the supreme
and final torture to which Winston is subjected. The
actual description of it is not one of the best things
in the book. A cage of hungry rats is attached to his
head in such a manner that when the door is opened
their only way out will be by eating through his face.
What snakes, spiders or weasels are to some people,
rats seem to have been to Orwell. In both *Homage to
Catalonia* and *Coming up for Air* he compares a man
flattening himself on the ground to escape gunfire to
a rat squeezing under a door, which suggests that he
had looked at rats more attentively than most people;
and in 1984 he builds up the horror of the final torture
by means of an incident earlier in the book in which
Winston nearly faints with disgust at the sight of a
rat. But the description of the torture is not very
successful. When we read:

> The rats knew what was coming now. One of them was
> leaping up and down, the other, an old scaly grandfa-

ther of the sewers, stood up, with his pink hands against
the bars, and fiercely snuffed the air—

we can hardly help being reminded of a schoolboy's
thriller.

But, successful or not as a description, the passage is
crucial, not only for 1984 but for the whole of Orwell's
work. It is the passage, referred to earlier in this book,
where Winston screams out: "Do it to Julia! Not me!"
—which is what the torturer O'Brien has wanted to
make him say. Long before he is threatened with the
rat torture he has been to all appearance broken, mentally as well as physically. He has signed every confes-
sion presented to him and incriminated everybody, including Julia; he has learned to believe, by means of
doublethink, that two and two can make five, that the
past is whatever the Party says it was and may at any
moment change, without changing, of course, because
it must always have been whatever the Party at any
moment says it was; and so on. But he has not betrayed Julia. He has incriminated her, of course; but
he still loves her, and is therefore still a rebel against
the Party, which tolerates no personal or private feelings. He will not be cured until all his love is for Big
Brother.

It is only when, in his terror of the rats, he has the
idea of interposing another human body, Julia's, for
them to devour while he shelters behind it, that he is
finally cured of his heresy. The cure consists in the
loss of his self-respect. He can no longer feel anything
for himself, for Julia, or for anyone. He feels he is
nothing, and in his nothingness he turns to Big
Brother as his only salvation.

THIS, as I read it, is Orwell's hard saying and his last
word. If you would not give your body to be devoured

for the sake of your loved one; if, on the contrary, you would shelter behind him or her, you are worth nothing. And so long as men are worth nothing, they will deserve and will get nothing better than conscious or unconscious slavery. It is such a hard saying that one instinctively feels there must be something wrong with it—morbidity, the feverishness of a sick man, spiritual pride? It is really the same idea as Kirilov's in *The Possessed*: that man can only cease to be a slave and become a god by killing himself, because "full freedom will come only when it makes no difference whether to live or not to live." But just as the power philosophy of the Party is presented in fantastic and almost hysterical terms, so one is tempted to say that there is something lurid and oversimplified about the final torture scene and its aftermath of total humiliation. Julia has been through similar tortures, with the same result, and when she and Winston meet again by chance they find they have no feeling at all for one another. Each of them has learned in the torture chamber that "all you care about is yourself."

The only way to criticize this conclusion, it seems to me, is to shake off the spell of Orwell's obsession and say that their real trouble was that they could not forgive themselves for not being superhumanly brave. There *is* in fact a touch of spiritual pride in the moral of the book. But in making this comment we put ourselves in the position of Sancho Panza criticizing Don Quixote. In his personal life Orwell was capable of Quixotic heroism; he made exorbitant demands upon himself, and no doubt he considered that he failed to live up to them. But like the rest of us he had to try to live with his failures, for I do not suppose that even he would have claimed that it is our duty to commit suicide as soon as we have discovered that we fall short of perfection. Indeed—leaving aside the apparent moral of 1984—I can think of hardly anyone who would have been less likely to say anything so silly. He had plenty of common sense and was often a very acute critic of overweeningly ambitious virtue.

During the last three years of his life he wrote two essays on this very theme: "Lear, Tolstoy and the Fool" and "Reflections on Gandhi" (both included in *Shooting an Elephant*). In the first he criticizes Tolstoy's attempt to renounce his worldly goods and in the second he discusses Gandhi's asceticism. Rather unexpectedly, he is more critical of Tolstoy than of Gandhi, but this is perhaps because he is discussing Tolstoy mainly in connection with his attack on Shakespeare. He points out, shrewdly enough, that the reason why Tolstoy was particularly irritated by *King Lear* may well have been because he saw it as a kind of parody of his own personal story, even including—though he could not have foreseen this—the final exodus from home and wandering to death. According to Orwell, what Shakespeare is, in effect, saying is: "Give away your lands if you want to, but don't expect to gain happiness by doing so. Probably you won't gain happiness. If you live for others, you must live *for others*, and not as a roundabout way of getting an advantage for yourself." A conclusion which Orwell thinks must have been displeasing to Tolstoy.

But did Tolstoy hope to "gain happiness" by renouncing the world? Was he, as Orwell suggests, practicing self-denial for selfish reasons? In order to be fair to Tolstoy we should need to analyze the word "happiness" in the way that Orwell analyzed "I want" in *The Road to Wigan Pier*: I don't want to cut down my drinking, pay my debts, etc.; but in another and more permanent sense I *do* want to do these things. There is also more than one sense of the word happiness. But the main burden of Orwell's criticism of both Tolstoy and Gandhi is that they were otherworldly; that is to say, they were anti-humanist. The purpose of their asceticism, he says, was to escape from suffering, and if carried to its logical conclusion it would bring the world to an end.

> If one could follow it to its psychological roots, one would, I believe, find that the main motive for "non-attachment" is a desire to escape from the pain of living, and above all from love, which, sexual or non-sexual, is hard work.—"Reflections on Gandhi"

In the last resort, he insists, one is either for God or for Man. One cannot be for both. And it is only those who choose Man who are really concerned about men's happiness in the world. But this is clearly untrue of some of the greatest saints, who became what they were precisely because they possessed—and exercised —an abnormally great capacity for love. "He that loveth not his brother whom he hath seen how can he love God whom he hath not seen?" This is a complete answer to Orwell's claim that we are compelled to choose between God and Man. And although it is true that in Gandhi's philosophy existence is an evil and escape from the wheel of existence is a good, it is obvious that in practice his life was almost entirely devoted to improving his countrymen's conditions of existence. Not very many humanistic reformers would go, as the otherworldly Gandhi did, to the length of personally cleaning out the latrines in pariah villages.*

It seems to me that Orwell was a good deal nearer to the otherworldly Tolstoy and Gandhi and a good

---

* See also A. J. Toynbee's criticism of Gibbon and Sir James Frazer in A Study of History and his quotation from Dawes and Baynes Three Byzantine Saints: "One of the outstanding features of early Byzantine asceticism is its passion for social justice and its championship of the poor and oppressed."

deal further from the average humanistic progressive than he himself was prepared to recognize.

> The essence of being human [he wrote in the "Reflections on Gandhi"] is that one does not seek perfection, that one *is* sometimes willing to commit sins for the sake of loyalty, that one does not push asceticism to the point where it makes friendly intercourse impossible, and that one is prepared in the end to be defeated and broken up by life, which is the inevitable price of fastening one's love upon other human individuals.

That is very well said, but he does not seem to have reflected that to be *prepared* to be defeated and broken up by life is already a step in the direction of non-attachment.

Winston and Julia in 1984 were in fact perfectly prepared, intellectually. They knew very well that their secret life together would certainly be discovered and that the end would be torture and submission. In Winston's own words: "On the battlefield, in the torture chamber, on a sinking ship, the issues that you are fighting for are always forgotten because the body swells up until it fills the universe." There may be some rare people of superhuman fortitude to whom this does not happen. But why should Winston have expected to be one of them? And if he did not expect this, why was his spirit broken for ever when he failed to resist under the torture, when he found himself wishing that Julia should be eaten by the rats? Speculation is difficult in such a matter, and perhaps everyone would be shattered as he was by such a revelation of our basic and absolute egocentricity; but it does seem at least possible that a less purely intellectual, a more *profound* non-attachment—which is perhaps only a way of saying a little more humility—might have helped him. Nearly all of us are failures, and we have to learn to live with our failure.

But the only thing that would certainly have enabled Winston to survive the shame of his collapse would have been the perfect humility defined by Simone Weil in her reflections on prayer:

> It means knowing that in the ego there is nothing whatever, no psychological element, which external circumstances could not make disappear. It means accepting that. It means being happy that it should be so.

Winston's love for Julia was the "psychological element" in his ego that he wished to cling to at all costs. The "external circumstance" of torture caused it to disappear. And he could not be happy that it was so. To achieve such perfectly humble resignation he would, of course, have needed to be a saint. But the achievement is at least psychologically conceivable. Orwell, however, requires him to possess such superhuman fortitude that no external circumstance whatever could obliterate his love. And this is probably impossible, and therefore not effectively conceivable at all.

THE FACT that Orwell chose to set the personal tragedy of Winston Smith at the center of his story is important as a clue to his own psychology. Winston's failure to rise to superhuman heroism, and the consequences of this failure, confirm the impression we derived from *A Clergyman's Daughter* that Orwell's motto should have been "all or nothing." But his prophecy is independent of the particular form in which he embodied it. He could have described the world of 1984 in exactly the same way without introducing any such character as Winston Smith. Nor, for that matter, is it essential that the ruling oligarchy should be a cruel and sadistic one. As we have already observed, Aldous Huxley's theory is equally plausible: that people can be reduced to a servile condition by means of mass suggestion, hypnopaedia and drugs, without any overt brutality or cruelty and without any conscious suffering. The core of Orwell's message in 1984, stripped of Winston's tragedy and all the sadism, is simply that our industrial machine civilization is tending to deracinate and debilitate us, and will finally destroy us; and the consensus of opinion on this point among thinkers as diverse as Orwell, Huxley, Gandhi, Simone Weil and D. H. Lawrence, to say nothing of the many others, such as Eliot and Koestler, who would go at least part of the way with them, is striking and depressing. All the more so because no one seriously believes that the rhythm of industrialization and mechanization could be relaxed, or indeed that it can possibly fail to go on accelerating (unless interrupted by war) until the whole population of the world has been incorporated into the mass civilization. Nor is it possible even to wish to reverse the process. Industrialization does seem to be the only way by which the conditions of the Asiatic coolie and the African tribesman can be raised to the level which is the prerequisite of anything that we in the West would consider a civilized or even a properly human life. "The belly comes before the soul, not in the scale of values but in point of time," as Orwell himself put it. And while there are still empty bellies to be filled one might as well whistle to the wind as make any reference to the complementary truth that it is possible to lose your soul in the process of gaining the world. Perhaps the only legitimate conclusion is Orwell's in *The Road to Wigan Pier*—"the machine has got to be accepted, but it is probably better to accept it rather as one accepts a drug—that is, grudgingly and suspiciously."

I SAID in Chapter 2 that Orwell was not interested in psychology or philosophy and that he seldom spoke of religion because he considered the word to have been fouled by centuries of hypocrisy. I did not say, however, that his mind was ill-equipped for dealing with these subjects. He sometimes makes very sound psychological observations, but they are thrown off casually and the implication seems to be that he has no time to go into the matter, which can, in any case, be taken as understood between all sensible men. And his much rarer references to religion are in the same vein. In his essay on Swift we find this:

> Part of our minds—in any normal person it is the dominant part—believes that man is a noble animal and life is worth living; but there is also a sort of inner self which at least intermittently stands aghast at the horror of existence. In the queerest way, pleasure and disgust are linked together.

But having noted something queer he immediately rises to the surface with a sane and humdrum conclusion: "The human body is beautiful: it is also repulsive and ridiculous, a fact which can be verified at any swimming pool."

And in the essay on Arthur Koestler he has this to say about religion:

> The only easy way out is that of the religious believer, who regards this life merely as a preparation for the next. But few thinking people now believe in life after death, and the number of them who do is probably diminishing. The Christian churches would probably not survive on their own merits if their economic basis were destroyed. The real problem is how to restore the religious attitude while accepting death as final. Men can only be happy when they do not assume that the object of life is happiness.

There is a brisk, dismissive, businesslike note in the remark about "accepting death as final." But words like "final" lose some of their briskness under philosophical inspection. Death is certainly final in the sense that it means your time has come, your time is up. But what *is* your time? And suppose Wittgenstein is right in saying that "the solution of the riddle of life in space and time lies *outside* space and time?" Orwell's reply to this might well be some polite variant of the Nietzschean *argumentum ad hominem:* That may be so, but why do *you* say it? And perhaps he would be justified, for it is certainly possible to use Wittgenstein's text as a pretext for all kinds of soulful escapism.

There are times, however, when his controversial manner becomes too summary and offhand. He can begin a sentence with "There seems to be good reason for believing . . ." and then announce some proposition which there is no reason at all for believing except that he happens to do so at the moment. On the other hand, his style can be deceptive. It is so swift and simple and unpretentious that his best arguments sometimes appear much easier and more obvious than they really are. In the "Reflections on Gandhi," for example, he praises Gandhi for assuming that all human beings are more or less approachable and will respond to a generous gesture, but then proceeds to question the assumption by pointing out that it is not necessarily true if you are dealing with lunatics. "Then the question becomes: Who is sane? Was Hitler sane? And is it not possible for one whole culture to be insane by the standards of another?" A more pompous and pretentious writer might take a whole chapter to make this point, and make it less effectively. (The point is, of course, developed at length in 1984. Winston Smith's sanity was insane by the Party's standards.)

NOT ALL the essays which seemed so fresh and original when they first appeared have worn very well; and just as *The English People* (1947) is lacking in vitality compared with *The Lion and the Unicorn,* so some of the later essays, beginning with the attack on Dali (1944), seem rather stereotyped. The study of Kipling (1942), however, is in places as vigorous and colorful as any he wrote. It claims, truly enough, that Kipling gave us almost the only readable account we possess of nineteenth-century Anglo-India and of the army which sustained it.

> It is a crude, vulgar picture, in which a patriotic music-hall turn seems to have got mixed up with one of Zola's gorier passages but from it future generations will be able to gather some idea of what a long-term volunteer army was like. . . . It took a very improbable combination of circumstances to produce Kipling's gaudy tableau, in which Private Ortheris and Mrs. Hauksbee pose against a background of palm trees to the sound of temple bells, and one necessary circumstance was that Kipling himself was only half civilised.

The technique of this essay is typical of Orwell's method. He admits and even emphasizes Kipling's vulgarity, sadism and sentimentality, but then turns upon his critics and rends them, pointing out that Kipling possessed, what so many progressive and supposedly enlightened people lack, namely, an understanding of the nature of responsibility. The people Kipling idealized, whatever their faults, were in the position of being responsible for getting things done. The Left Wing critics who attack Kipling can indulge in idealistic heroics precisely because they are usually not in positions of responsibility.

In one form or another, Orwell returned to this point again and again. We all like to assume attitudes of noble disinterestedness, even—or perhaps especially—when this involves despising the very people whose work makes our comfortable superiority possible; and we become schizophrenic (which is the technique of *doublethink*) when the true facts of the situation are forced upon us. Thus, in "Notes on Nationalism" he reminds pacifists that: "Those who 'abjure' violence can only do so because others are committing violence on their behalf," and in "Anti-Semitism in Britain" he observes that: "Plenty of people who are quite capable of being objective about sea-urchins, say, or the square root of 2, become schizophrenic if they have to think about the sources of their own income." The argument of the "Notes on Nationalism" is important and profound and it is a great pity he was never able to develop it more fully. He distinguishes between patriotism and nationalism, defining patriotism as "devotion to a particular place and a particular way of life, which one believes to be the best in the world but has no wish to force upon other people." To the word nationalism he gives a much broader definition than the usual one. It is made to include not only ordinary Jingoism, but Communism, Trotskyism, Nazism, political Catholicism, Pacifism, Anti-Semitism, Zionism and the Celtic nationalisms. His excuse for thus overworking the word is that there exists no other convenient one for the phenomenon under consideration. This phenomenon is a modern disease, a sort of cancer-growth of the will to power.

> The abiding purpose of every nationalist is to secure more power and more prestige, *not* for himself but for the nation or other unit in which he has chosen to sink his own individuality.

This definition is a good example of Orwell's deceptively simple profundity, though unfortunately it cannot be said that he ever adequately developed this conception of nationalism, either in this essay or anywhere else. Its essence is the sinking of one's individu-

ality in some group or cause or movement with the
consequence that one becomes licensed to act *and
think* in ways which would not be permissible or even
possible for a responsible independent individual. The
cause justifies and covers everything. This is, in fact,
precisely the aberration which Simone Weil describes
as *idolatry*. But Orwell was no theologian and he
confined himself to examining some of the consequences of idolatrous self-surrender or nationalism.
He was well aware, of course, that almost everyone
who honestly examines his own mind will find in it
some traces of nationalistic mania, either religious,
racial, political or social; but his strength was in the
fact that he was about as free from it as anyone can
be and was therefore able to detect an exceptionally
wide range of specimens. Here he is describing the
consequences of some of the more obvious ones:

> For quite six years the English admirers of Hitler con-
> trived not to learn of the existence of Dachau and
> Buchenwald. And those who were loudest in denounc-
> ing the German concentration camps were often quite
> unaware, or only very dimly aware, that there are also
> concentration camps in Russia. Huge events like the
> Ukraine famine of 1933, involving the deaths of mil-
> lions of people, have actually escaped the attention of
> the majority of English Russophiles. Many English peo-
> ple heard almost nothing about the extermination of
> German and Polish Jews during the war. Their own
> anti-Semitism has caused this vast crime to bounce off
> their consciousness. In nationalist thought there are
> facts which are both true and untrue, known and un-
> known. A known fact may be so unbearable that it is
> habitually pushed aside and not allowed to enter into
> logical processes, or on the other hand it may enter into
> every calculation and yet never be admitted as a fact,
> even in one's own mind. . . . In 1927 Chiang Kai Shek
> boiled hundreds of Communists alive, and yet within

ten years he had become one of the heroes of the Left. The realignment of world politics had brought him into the anti-Fascist camp and so it was felt that the boiling of the Communists "didn't count," or perhaps had not happened.

Had he lived, Orwell could have expanded this passage, since a more recent "realignment of world politics" has brought Chiang Kai Shek back once again into the anti-Communist camp.

The preceding extract gives, I think, a fair example of the style of Orwell's later essays. Another good example is "The Prevention of Literature," which he wrote some time between 1945 and 1949. Like the nationalism essay, it covers too much ground with a too great apparent ease, which tends to mask the deep feeling behind it and may cause a reader to miss seeing the full horror of the all too probable prediction it makes:

> Probably novels and stories will be completely superseded by film and radio productions. Or perhaps some kind of low-grade sensational fiction will survive, produced by a sort of conveyor-belt process that reduces human initiative to the minimum.
>
> It would probably not be beyond human ingenuity to write books by machinery. But a sort of mechanising process can already be seen at work in the film and radio, in publicity and propaganda, and in the lower reaches of journalism. The Disney films, for instance, are produced by what is essentially a factory process . . .

Again one is reminded of his advice in *The Road to Wigan Pier* that the machine should be accepted in the same way that one accepts a drug—reluctantly and grudgingly. The idea that books could be assembled and produced by conveyor belt is used in *1984*, where Julia works as a mechanic on the novel-writing machines.

It is remarkable how many of his chief preoccupations Orwell managed to pack into 1984. A major one toward the end of his life was the connection between language and morality. Official euphemisms fitted together into prefabricated sentences can not only save the speaker from the trouble of thinking but can actually deaden his consciousness of what he is really saying. Keep your English simple, says Orwell; refuse to learn any of the official jargons, and then at least if you make a stupid remark its stupidity will be obvious, even to yourself. He gives a more sinister example of the abuse of language when he asks us to consider some comfortable English professor defending Russian totalitarianism in the following terms:

> While freely conceding that the Soviet regime exhibits certain features which the humanitarian may be inclined to deplore, we must, I think, agree that a certain curtailment of the right to political opposition is an unavoidable concomitant of transitional periods, and that the rigours which the Russian people have been called upon to undergo have been amply justified in the sphere of concrete achievement.
>   —"Politics and the English Language"

He then offers an English translation:

> I believe in killing off your opponents when you can get good results by doing so.

So really the most alarming character in 1984 is not Big Brother, or O'Brien with his cage of rats; it is the man from the Fiction Department whose interminable flow of talk gets on Winston's nerves during lunch in the canteen.

He was a man of about thirty, with a muscular throat and a large mobile mouth. His head was thrown back a little, and because of the angle at which he was sitting, his spectacles caught the light and presented to Winston two blank discs instead of eyes. . . . As he watched the eyeless face with the jaw moving rapidly up and down, Winston had a curious feeling that this was not a real human being but some kind of dummy. It was not the man's brain that was speaking, it was his larynx. The stuff that was coming out of him consisted of words, but it was not speech, in the true sense; it was a noise uttered in unconsciousness, like the quacking of a duck.

POSSIBLY the appalling office jargon used in the Ministry of Truth was suggested to Orwell by the code in which newspaper correspondents cable their dispatches. For example, Winston Smith receives the following instruction:

times 3.12. 83 reporting bb dayorder doubleplusungood refs unpersons rewrite fullwise upsub antefiling.

In standard English:

The reporting of Big Brother's Order for the Day in the *Times* of December 3rd 1983 is extremely unsatisfactory and makes references to non-existent persons [i.e. persons who have since been liquidated]. Rewrite it in full and submit your draft to higher authority before filing.

The justification for the "cablese" used by journalists in real life is, of course, economy and speed in cabling; but it may well produce in the long run the sort of effect which Orwell foresaw. I was once in a town where some refugees who had been granted asylum were to be officially welcomed. A correspondent of my acquaintance had to cable an account of their reception to a newspaper, according to whose policy the refugees should be enthusiastically received. His message ran something like this: "in brilliant sunshine while bells pealed etband played party refugees welcomed parmonster demo unions cumsalvoes rockets etflags etembraces stop banners read quote hail heroes unquote stop addresses parprominentest reps govt cumgensecy paraphrasing leaflets cumtext quote welcome dear guests. . . ." and so on.

Another newspaper reported in a headline: "CROWD'S CHILLY WELCOME," and a third reported that "the populace refused to respond to the cheers of the refugees." I did not see the cables upon which these statements were based, but it is possible to reconcile the divergent pictures, up to a point, by distinguishing between the unorganized crowd on the one hand and the organized trade-union demonstration on the other—though there would still be room for argument as to what constitutes a *monster* demo." But the point is that the authors of all three accounts were probably not expected by their employers to make any attempt to give an accurate description of the event. They were technicians on a job, and the jobs happened to be different. One of them had to boost the occasion up and the others had to write it down. It is probably easier to carry out that sort of assignment in a technical jargon than in plain English.

The press and the other modern techniques of mass suggestion have great hypnotic power. Perhaps, after all, Orwell was not so unrealistic in imagining a civilized nation reduced permanently to a helpless and demoralized mob; and it may be that my criticism on page 97–98 is much too complacent.

LITERARY HISTORY

. . . verminous little lions.
—From *The Road to Wigan Pier*

WHAT IS ORWELL'S POSITION today among twentieth-century men of letters? From one point of view he belongs with Malraux, Koestler and Silone, representatives of what he himself described, in his essay on Koestler in 1944, as "the special class of literature that has arisen out of the European political struggle since the rise of Fascism." (He does not mention Bernanos, who should be included, but adds two historians, Salvemini and Borkenau.) As an Englishman, he is a unique specimen of the type. English critics of fascism and communism have usually known the evils they spoke of only by report and at a distance; and those who wished to praise one brand of totalitarianism while denouncing the other had little difficulty, because it is as easy to imagine the virtues as the vices in a system of which one has no personal knowledge. But Orwell, whether he wrote of poverty or of political persecution, was always talking of what he knew about from personal experience. As the only English novelist of the three, it is characteristic that he should be more of an artist and less of a philosopher than either Malraux or Koestler. *La Condition Humaine* and *Darkness at Noon* are overwhelmingly impressive books, but *Animal Farm*, although so much smaller, is a more complete work of art.

But to think of Orwell primarily as a member of this group is to miss a part of his significance. It places him correctly for the period in which those writers were, so to speak, the conscience-keepers of the intellectual élite of Europe. Orwell himself can be said to have held this position for the English intellectuals from the time of the Spanish war, through the second world war and up to the beginning of the cold war. But we need to place him in a different perspective in order to distinguish the qualities which have earned for him the high standing which he still maintains more than ten years after his death. It is a question whether his comparatively small literary output would suffice, by itself, to support the unique position he occupies. But before trying to answer this question it is necessary to trace a brief outline sketch of English social-literary history during the last fifty years.

IN 1915, after more than a dozen years of precarious mutual esteem and admiration, Henry James and H. G. Wells had a quarrel. To investigate all the implications of this quarrel would require many volumes, in addition to the interesting one already devoted to it by Messrs. Leon Edel and Gordon N. Ray. But for our present purpose H. G. Wells provided a useful clue when he wrote to James: "I have set before myself a gamin-esque ideal." He was attempting to excuse himself for having ridiculed James in a book entitled *Boon*; and he went on to explain that he had felt it necessary, precisely because of his great admiration for James, to emphasize sharply his disagreement with what he regarded as James's art for art's sake principles. He had felt he must hit back hard in order to avoid being overwhelmed. But by 1915 Wells himself was already famous and far more widely read than Henry James. The truth is that he was exhibiting a delayed "angry young man" reaction against a literary "Establishment" personified, in his eyes, by James.

It was a considerably delayed reaction because, in fact, the progressive movement associated with the names of Shaw and Wells had been in the ascendant for some time. However, the sense of being a pioneer is apt to survive the actuality and it is of course true that Wells himself had had a real struggle to get even the necessary minimum of education. For the rest of his life, despite his colossal success and world-wide fame, he carried a chip on his shoulder. It can be seen again in his relations with Joseph Conrad, so well described by Conrad's biographer, Mr. Jocelyn Baines. Note particularly Wells's irritated description in his autobiography of "Conrad's *persona* of a romantic adventurous un-mercenary intensely artistic European gentleman carrying an exquisite code of unblemished honour through a universe of baseness . . ." But with all his *gaminesquerie*, Wells's influence upon his age was unquestionably beneficial and liberating. The movement in which he was a leader included the rise of the Labour Party and the first challenge of Science to the monopolistic prestige of the Classics in education; and it is no wonder that it attracted to itself so great a part of the imaginative, intelligent and generous youth of the age. Although there remained, of course, some important literary influences outside and unconnected with the movement—Belloc and Chesterton, representing a progressive and even revolutionary Catholic conservatism; Kipling, who was unique; and Conrad, who carried on the tradition of Henry James—it was undoubtedly Wells and Shaw who represented the main intellectual current of the times.

Inevitably, having put socialism on the political

map, brought education up to date, won the vote for women, and swept away tons of Victorian lumber, the progressive movement began to show signs of wear and tear. Some of its effects upon the minds of bright young people were seen to be not entirely good. Among these questionable effects was the encouragement of a shallow, hedonistic, and completely unrealistic optimism about scientific progress and human perfectibility, and of an ignorant and arrogant contempt for tradition and the past, and for cultures uninfluenced by the Western scientific spirit.

With thinkers like T. E. Hulme and T. S. Eliot a reaction set in; and from the end of the first world war until the outbreak of the second, twenty-one years later, the social-literary history of England consisted largely of the gradual transference of prestige from the optimistic humanism of the progressive movement to a somewhat disillusioned and austere traditionalism. But once again there are some important literary figures who do not fit into the general picture: for example, Aldous Huxley, D. H. Lawrence, Middleton Murry, and Orwell.* None of these four could be described as traditionalist but, though all of them directly or indirectly owed a great deal to Shaw and Wells, none of them could be described as progressive in the Shavian or Wellsian senses of the word.

And yet Orwell, as was pointed out in Chapter 2, is in the direct line of descent of "angry young men" between H. G. Wells and John Osborne. The new class of young writers of whom John Osborne was at one time considered to be typical—although he is in fact an original and not a type, and although many of

* A very incomplete list, of course; but I am only trying to present a diagram, not an accurate picture, and I claim the diagrammatist's license to distort. Some important writers—Herbert Read, for example, or F. R. Leavis—would be difficult to place.

the class do not even resemble him in being angry— are a phenomenon dating from the end of the second world war. Sociologically, they represent the effects of the great expansion of higher education in the years between the emergence of H. G. Wells and the present day, and the fulfilment of a good many of the ideals of the progressive movement. Yet they find themselves confronted with a literary Establishment in some ways not very different from the one which Wells was attacking in his controversy with Henry James. As a class these young intellectuals, with rare exceptions, show very little sign of the direct influence of either Shaw or Wells, and even less of Huxley or Murry; but they owe a good deal to D. H. Lawrence, and perhaps even more to Orwell. Their literary performances to date do not suggest that these influences, or the proportions in which they have imbibed them, are necessarily the ideal ones. But in so far as they admire Orwell, they appear to do so for the right reasons.

BEFORE EXAMINING the reasons for which Orwell is admired, it is necessary to study a little more closely his relationship to the three writers with whom we have grouped him, very incongruously it may seem, as standing somewhat apart from the scientific, humanistic, progressive movement which was in the ascendant during the first three or four decades of the century, and also from the more traditionalist and conservative movement which challenged it from about 1918 onward. In spite of the striking differences between them, there are three points upon which Lawrence, Murry, Huxley and Orwell are agreed. They perceive, in Orwell's words, that "men can only be happy when they do not assume that the object of life is happiness." They hold, again as Orwell puts it that it is necessary "to restore the religious attitude."

And they agree in not looking to orthodox Christianity for the inspiration of the religious attitude which they wish to restore. After that the divergencies between them become considerable, but it must be admitted that their basic points of agreement are not trivial.

Being all of them literary artists or critics, or both, and not technical philosophers or theologians, their statements about their fundamental beliefs do not lend themselves to neat classification or definition. But Aldous Huxley for one, is not difficult to classify. He has done all he could to make it clear that he believes in the tradition of the "perennial philosophy," the religion of the mystics which is mysteriously similar, *semper et ubique*, in China, in India, in Persia, and in both Pagan and Christian Europe. Both Huxley and Murry were deeply influenced by Lawrence, but Murry was by far the more tenacious in trying to grasp what Lawrence meant and to reconcile it with his own unorthodox Christianity. Lawrence alone of the four, and perhaps alone among English writers of this century, was a man of indisputably great genius and was also by far the most original and the hardest to understand. He claimed only to be trying to revive a kind of religious insight which the modern world had lost. But to his critics he seemed to be trying— pathetically, outrageously, or heroically, according to the critic's bias—to *create* the religion of which he believed the world was in need.

And Orwell? Beyond the two statements already quoted and the addendum that "death is final" it is not easy to find any statement of his fundamental beliefs. He differs from the other three in having less literary genius than Lawrence and less intellectual brilliancy than Huxley or Murry. But he has a compensating advantage in that he is more down to earth, more realistic; he has more of the common touch. It is true that, compared to Lawrence, his ability to *understand* the common man was very limited. But, on the other hand, he felt more *at home* with him. Both Orwell and Huxley might at one time have been said to show, as opposed to Lawrence and Murry, a strong affinity with eighteenth-century rationalism. Huxley's early writings are full of Voltairian skepticism and flippancy, but the influence of Lawrence and later of mysticism wrought a complete change; whereas Orwell, who never showed any signs of flippancy, was always more or less faithful to the hard-headed, if one-eyed, rationalism of the Enlightenment.

He does, however, on two occasions say that it is desirable to restore "the religious attitude" though he rules out Christianity on account of its belief in personal immortality, which, as he probably correctly thought, is more and more losing its hold upon thinking people. In an article on "The Christian Reformers" in the *Manchester Evening News* (February 7, 1946) he discusses sympathetically the social opinions of Maritain and Berdyaev and praises Belloc's "very prescient book" *The Servile State;* and in a subsequent article on pacifists he gives a remarkably clear and fair statement of the case for Pacifism. In particular he discusses, not without sympathy but with doubts, the pacifist's answer to the charge that non-resistance helps a tyrannical government and weakens a liberal one. The intelligent pacifist, he says, will admit that his policy may at first seem to make evil stronger, but will claim that it is nevertheless the only way to defeat the philosophy of government by coercion: the first step toward sanity is to break the cycle of violence. In this article he discusses the social attitude of Aldous Huxley and Murry but, as with Berdyaev and Maritain, he steers clear of their religious views. The truth is, I believe, that he did not want to think too deeply about what he called "other-worldliness" as opposed to the "this-worldliness" of the socialist who is concerned to make men's earthly life happier. He must have known, though he preferred not to discuss the point, that there exist many "religious attitudes" unconnected with a belief in personal immortality. An elementary knowledge of Buddhist philosophy, which he certainly possessed, is sufficient to establish the point. Nor would he have found much about personal immortality in the writings of Huxley or Murry. (What, indeed, did Orwell mean—what does anybody mean—by personal immortality? Who, or what, is the "person"? And can anyone really desire or conceive the possibility of becoming an immortal person?) What he might have found, if he had pursued the subject, is that this-worldliness and other-worldliness are not so incompatible as he claimed. He might even have found that they existed together, in a very perfect balance, among his own fundamental beliefs.

ORWELL's social irreconcilability up to the age of thirty-three is distinguished from the angry rebellion of most young men by the high degree of its disinterestedness. He was in rebellion not because he felt deprived and thwarted, but because Asiatic coolies, tramps and down-and-outs were oppressed and despised. (Why are beggars despised? he asked, and gave the answer: Solely because begging is not a profitable business.) And whatever decision Orwell made— whether it was to rebel, or to fight, or to investigate poverty—he went the whole way. I believe his wholeheartedness is one of the things he is admired for.

But this is a moral quality, and a good man does not necessarily write good books. Indeed, can we even be sure that it is impossible for a thoroughly *bad* man to write good books?

If I have any sophisticated readers, I suppose they can hardly wait to point out that I am asking a meaningless question. I am not so sure. But no doubt it is a question that would need an intolerable amount of refining and qualifying before it could even begin to be seriously discussed. One thing, however, is certain: there does exist a type of good book whose goodness is directly or indirectly, obviously or subtly, connected with certain moral excellences in the writer. It is also true that certain types of behavior which, according to the wisdom of the world, appear gratuitous, unbalanced, and masochistic are in some cases an indication of an exceptional moral stature; and in such cases the people who exhibit the behavior become endowed with a sort of authority which somehow makes itself felt in their words.

Both Simone Weil and Orwell are cases in point. Simone Weil's limiting her expenses to the weekly strike pay of the strikers at Le Puy, her wearing herself out in the Renault factory and in the vineyard; Orwell's dish-washing, hop-picking, and sleeping in doss houses; the strangely similar experiences of each of them in the Spanish civil war—nothing, it might seem, could be more futile and wasteful of their talents. Yet even on the simple controversial level their strange and original attitude to life gave them a certain advantage.

In her *Memoirs of a Dutiful Daughter* Simone de Beauvoir tells, with characteristic objectivity and magnanimity, a story against herself about her meeting with Simone Weil. These two young girls were the two most brilliant philosophy students of their year, and one day Mlle. de Beauvoir approached Mlle. Weil, who was holding forth "in no uncertain tones," in the courtyard of the Sorbonne. Politics was Mlle. Weil's theme and she was asserting

that only one thing mattered in the world today: the Revolution which would feed all the starving people of the earth. I retorted, no less peremptorily, that the problem was not to make men happy, but to find the reason for their existence. She looked me up and down: "It's easy to see you've never gone hungry," she snapped.

There is a comparable passage in Orwell's "Inside the Whale." Returning to England from Spain, he reads a poem on the subject of the civil war, in which he had recently been wounded, and he takes strong exception to a certain line in it. The poem, which in many ways he admires, is intended to emphasize the drab and tedious aspects of the revolutionary struggle. Poets are warned, in verse, that they must be prepared to put their poetic talents in cold storage and occupy themselves with ephemeral pamphlets and boring meetings. They must also make "the conscious acceptance of guilt in the necessary murder." This is too much for Orwell, whom it probably reminds of the murders in Barcelona when his P.O.U.M. and "Trotskyist" friends were liquidated by the Stalinists.

"All very edifying" he comments. "But notice the phrase 'necessary murder'. . . . The Hitlers and Stalins find murder necessary, but they don't advertise their callousness, and they don't speak of it as murder; it is 'liquidation' or 'elimination' or some other soothing phrase." This outspokenly callous poetic amoralism, he concludes "is only possible if you are the kind of person who is always somewhere else when the trigger is pulled."

Coming from Simone Weil and Orwell these retorts are not merely smart debating points. They have weight.

But in addition to their self-inflicted ordeals Simone Weil and Orwell have another point in common. As was shown in Chapter 1, they shared the same conception of Justice as the seeker of balance, with its corollary that the just man must always be prepared to flee from the camp of victory and join the weaker side. It is this characteristic of Orwell's that has led to misrepresentation of his political position. His socialist admirers have sometimes felt called upon to defend him against a charge of showing animus against the Left—though it would be more to the point to demonstrate that the Right has sometimes illegitimately claimed him as a supporter. But in any case he is in no need of this sort of defence, and those who attempt it merely show that they have failed to understand his essay on nationalism. Orwell was a socialist, but his socialism was not nationalistic in the sense of that essay; he did not belong to the school of "My Socialism right or wrong." On the contrary, since socialism was his faith he brought an exceptionally severe scrutiny to any nationalistic distortion of it; and of course in a world of competing nationalisms to criticize one form of nationalism will always be interpreted as supporting another. Orwell would have been astonished and indignant to know that 1984 was going to be interpreted by some anti-socialists in both America and England as a satire upon the British Labour government. If he ever criticized the Labour Party it was because of weaknesses in it which he feared would make it less able to prevent the coming of Big Brother. He criticized other parties and policies for the same reason. But not being a Labour nationalist, if he found any other party or policy which seemed more likely to lead people toward freedom and justice and away from the horrors of 1984 he would have supported it. Having found none, he continued to support the Labour Party, but critically. Nationalists, of course, are not good at taking criticism, which they confuse with hostility and opposition.

It is curious—or perhaps not so very curious—that Orwell himself has become for some people the object of a nationalistic cult. He might well have included this kind of personal cult in his list of nationalisms. Members of these cults adopt a possessive attitude toward their hero, resent the praise of any other hero, and regard any criticism of their own as a proof of enmity. At the present time both D. H. Lawrence and Orwell are the objects of this sort of cult.

TO RETURN to the question of whether Orwell's comparatively small output (eight full-length books, three short books and four books of essays) is sufficiently impressive to explain by itself the high standing and influence which he still enjoys. I think it is doubtful. I think his eminence is partly due to the fact that "first he wrought and afterwards he taught." The reader knows that the man who wrote the books lived and acted in a certain way and this reacts upon his feeling about the books. But I also believe that this tells us more about the age we live in than about Orwell's literary potentialities. There is no doubt that he was by nature "a born writer," and he himself knew it; but he lived at a time when any man with the character and gifts which might make him a first-rate literary artist would be unlikely to devote his gifts exclusively to writing. Moreover, he was not, like some consumptive literary artists, precociously brilliant. Unlike Keats, Katherine Mansfield and D. H. Lawrence, he matured slowly; and the age of thirty-three, at which he might have begun to show his true powers, was precisely the age at which—to quote a *Punch* joke which seems to have amused him—he decided to give up the activity of "just *writing*" and begin "writing *about*" something. (The joke: "And what are you going to write about, dear?" "My dear Aunt, one doesn't write *about* anything. One just *writes*.") What he decided to write about was politics, and from then on, although he was still certainly a literary artist, it was more in the sense that one can apply the term to Swift, for example, than to Turgenev (whom, incidentally, I doubt if Orwell appreciated).

Had he been able to live a quiet and studious life, it is not easy to guess what sort of books he would have written. Judging by his attitude to David Jones's *In Parenthesis*, of which, although he admired the book, he complained that the writing was "mannered," and to *The Great Gatsby*, which, astonishingly, he found "lacking in point," I think that even in a quieter and less problematic age his interest would have been drawn to positive and even public problems and away from sensitive subjectivity, which he would have considered morbid. He would have resembled Ibsen or Gissing rather than Proust or Virginia Woolf; but he might well have developed his gift for humor and even farce. But these are only speculations, and are based upon nothing more solid than occasional remarks he made. I am convinced, however, that in spite of his admiration for Eliot and his considerable interest in Joyce and Yeats, his real affinity was rather with Dickens.

It is significant that he was much more interested in Conrad than in Henry James; and I believe there is an explanation which may appear superficial but is nevertheless true. Conrad's characters, in *Under Western Eyes*, and *The Secret Agent* as much as in *Lord Jim*, *Nostromo*, *Typhoon* and *The Shadow Line*, are dealing with problems that interested Orwell—anarchism, revolution, leadership, dangers, physical hardships; whereas the world of Henry James—millionaires, art collectors, gold diggers, intellectuals, social climbers—was antipathetic to him. It may have been for the same reason that he found *The Great Gatsby* lacking in point.

These considerations might seem to indicate a certain simplicity in Orwell, but he was really not so simple. It was rather that his writing always had a purpose—a political purpose, as he himself said. And an overriding purpose imposes certain limitations. Orwell accepted these limitations and was content to work within them; and what he lost in breadth he gained in depth. The reason why his books are still alive and seminal, when so many portentous works of socialist and Marxist propaganda have been forgotten, is that he dealt with permanent as well as with temporary problems. When economic and political and social conditions change, the work of the ephemeral propagandist becomes out of date. Neither fascism nor even unemployment is any longer the overwhelming menace it was in the nineteen-thirties; the issue of private capitalism versus nationalization in industry and the problems of imperialism and colonialism no longer appear in the same form. But Orwell's preoccupation with the danger of the servile State and his championship of individual liberty and justice and human decency are still as relevant as they ever were.

> *It is almost impossible to be honest and to remain alive.*
> —From *The Road to Wigan Pier*

IT IS UNSATISFACTORY, at least for biographical pur-
poses, to have a memory that records general situa-
tions, moods and states of mind, but not concrete
facts. Thus it was possible for me to know Orwell for
twenty years and yet to remember very few definite
facts about him. I know from records, not memory,
that I probably first met him in 1930, when he was 27
and I was three years older. I was then working with
Middleton Murry on *The Adelphi*, which was a quar-
terly at the time; and in the March–May issue we published a review of Lewis Mumford's *Herman Melville*
by E. A. Blair. After that, reviews, articles and, occa-
sionally, poems by him appeared fairly often, usually
signed Eric Blair until 1935. In April, 1931, we published "The Spike," which later formed part of *Down
and Out in Paris and London*. I remember talking
with him in a New Oxford Street tea-shop near our
Bloomsbury office. He made a pleasant impression
and I did not guess that he was having a struggle to
live, though he struck me as rather lacking in vitality.
It came out that we had been at the same school,
Eton, though the difference in our ages had prevented
our knowing one another. I do not remember if it also

came out that he had been there on a scholarship, but if it did he must certainly have been embarrassed and I equally certainly was unaware of his embarrassment.

A word of explanation may be necessary here. There are about a thousand boys at Eton, of whom about seventy are "King's Scholars" and live in the College proper. The remainder are called "Oppidans" and live in houses supervised by Housemasters. The scholars pay lower fees than the oppidans and in class and chapel they wear academic gowns over their black Eton suits. These are the only differences, except of course that the scholars are as a rule cleverer and work harder than the average oppidan—which would tend, or did in my day, to make them unpopular with the unintellectual majority. But I don't think that any *social* snobbery was involved. Aristocratic parents whose boys were clever enough to win scholarships quite often sent them to College. And, moreover, the disapproval of the majority was extended also to any oppidans who showed much interest in the lessons. But Eton is a tolerant school, and the disapproval was only mild. On account of the gowns they wore, the scholars were known as "Tugs" (from *toga*). So far from being despised, I should say that by the more intelligent and serious-minded oppidans they were rather admired.

But this evidently had not been Orwell's feeling. One day in 1948, when I had known him for eighteen years, I incautiously used the word "Tug" and although he was too polite to say anything he winced as if I had trodden on his tenderest corn. That a famous middle-aged writer should have retained such a deep trace of boyhood sensitiveness and suffering seems remarkable.

Between 1930 and 1935, if my memory is accurate, Orwell lived mainly in or near London, and his first job was at the school in the western outer suburbs which he pillories in *The Clergyman's Daughter*. Later he worked in a bookshop in Hampstead; and later still, when he married in 1936, he took a cottage, which was also the village shop, at Wallington in Hertfordshire. The plan was to run it as a general store, open afternoons only, so that he could write in the mornings. This was the beginning of his more cheerful period. But the poem "On a Ruined Farm near the His Master's Voice Gramophone Factory" (*Adelphi*, April, 1934) was undoubtedly suggested by the landscape around the detested school:

> *The acid smoke has soured the fields,*
> *And browned the few and windworn flowers—*

Nevertheless, Orwell certainly knew how to keep his bitterness to himself. During the five years when, on the evidence of his novels, his mood was so black and his circumstances so penurious, he was always a friendly, considerate and amiable companion. If one had been asked to describe him one would have said first of all that he gave the impression of absolute reliability and of lacking completely the jealous, pushful, intriguing, self-centered mentality which is so common among young ambitious literary men. He was obviously intelligent and able, but did not seem especially original or gifted. His novels seem to me better today than I thought them when they appeared in 1934, 1935, and 1936. In those days "experimental" and surrealist prose was fashionable, and Orwell's writing seemed rather stodgy and old-fashioned. He himself, indeed, seemed rather old-fashioned.

The Adelphi did not encourage surrealist prose, but it did publish a good many of the new intellectual Leftist poets whose verses Cyril Connolly parodied so well:

M *is for Marx*
and Movement of Masses
and Massing of Arses
and Clashing of Classes.

Compared with these excited young men Orwell seemed quite tame, and this in spite of the fact that one knew he had really lived among the proletariat instead of merely writing poems about it; and in spite of incidents like the following. He came to my flat one day and asked if he might change his clothes. Having left his respectable suit in the bedroom, he went off again dressed more or less in rags. He wanted, he said, to know about prison from the inside and he hoped that if he were picked up drunk and disorderly in the East End he might manage to achieve this. Next day he reappeared very crestfallen. He had duly got drunk and been taken to a police station. But once there he had received a fatherly talk, spent the night in a cell and been let out next morning with a cup of tea and some good advice.

I HAVE SAID that Orwell seemed rather old-fashioned, and the truth is that in many ways he *was* old-fashioned. He once said to me, *à propos* of nothing, so far as I can remember: "I hope you love your family?" I may be wrong in thinking there had been nothing to lead up to this remark, but in any case I knew him well enough to be able to interpret it. He was thinking of the Oedipus complex, the fear of castration by the father or absorption by the possessive mother and all the other psychological bogeys that have inspired so much of modern art and literature, and he was repudiating them. Rashly perhaps, because he was not always completely successful in loving his own family. He was estranged from his father for a number of years, and I can understand that the elder

Mr. Blair may have felt that he had reasonable grounds for complaint. A retired Indian civil servant cannot be expected to enjoy seeing his son become a voluntary down-and-out. But they were reconciled before his father's death, as Orwell told me with deep satisfaction, adding that he himself had closed his father's eyes in the traditional way by placing pennies upon the eyelids. He further added that after the funeral he had been embarrassed to know what to do with the pennies. "In the end I walked down to the sea and threw them in. Do you think some people would have put them back in their pocket?"

The only direct reference I ever heard him make to psychoanalysis was when he said: "A psychoanalyst would need to be cleverer than his patients." Upon which I made the obvious comment that there are many different *kinds* of cleverness, and he replied: "I mean cleverer in regard to the matters under discussion." And there was nothing more to be got out of him. But once again his thought is easy to interpret, and it goes to the root of the matter. The relation of father confessor and penitent in religion is governed by a tradition which transcends their personal characteristics and makes any question of their relative "cleverness" irrelevant. But it seems to require considerable assurance on the part of a psychoanalyst to rely upon his own skill in using a modern technique in order to enlighten other people upon the workings of the psyche, or soul. Orwell's thought, in fact, is closely related to that of Lise in *The Brothers Karamazov* when she is plotting with Alyosha to persuade Captain Snegiryov to accept some money while at the same time restoring his self-respect. "Aren't we showing contempt for him," she says, "for that poor man—in analysing his soul like this, as it were from above, eh? In deciding so certainly that he will take the money?" Beneath Orwell's bluntness and hostility to psychologizing there was a delicacy of feeling which a great many confidently subtle psychological artists conspicuously lack. (Note, for example, in *Homage to Catalonia*, his concern about the boy who was wrongly accused of stealing.)

When he went in 1936 to the distressed areas of Lancashire and Yorkshire to collect material for *The Road to Wigan Pier* he made use of several addresses I had given him. These were of trade unionists and local socialist leaders with whom I had come in contact through *The Adelphi*, and some of them wrote to me after his visit. An extremely respectable Catholic trade-union official in Manchester told me that Orwell arrived at his house having walked the last part of the journey. He and his wife had been shocked—and I think really almost alarmed—to learn that their guest had spent the previous night at a workhouse en route.

And a friend in Sheffield who had introduced him to a militant Communist propagandist told me the following story. The Communist started in on his routine vilification of the bourgeoisie, but was interrupted by Orwell who said: "Look here, I'm a bourgeois and my family are bourgeois. If you talk about them like that I'll punch your head."

IT WAS, HOWEVER, only when he went to Spain with his wife not long after their marriage and then disappeared into the militia that I began to realize he was extraordinary. Although I already knew him well, he had not seemed to be the sort of person who would do anything so dramatic. *The Road to Wigan Pier*, which I read a few months later, confirmed the impression that he was a more original and dynamic character than his ordinary everyday manner revealed. It is true that in the summer of 1936, some months before he went to Spain, he had attended a summer school organized by *The Adelphi*, where he astonished everybody, including the Marxist theoreticians, by his interventions in the discussions. Without any parade of learning he produced breathtaking Marxist paradoxes and epigrams, in such a way as to make the sacred mysteries seem almost too obvious and simple. At one of the sessions I noticed a leading Marxist eyeing him with a mixture of admiration and uneasiness.

When I passed through Barcelona in April, 1937, just before the street fighting and the liquidation of the P.O.U.M., I called on Orwell's wife, Eileen, at the P.O.U.M. office where she was working, and found her in what struck me as a very strange mental state. She seemed absent-minded, preoccupied, and dazed. As Orwell was at the front I assumed that it was worry about him that was responsible for her curious manner. But when she began talking about the risk, for me, of being seen in the street with her, that explanation no longer seemed to fit. In reality, of course, as I realized afterward, she was the first person in whom I had witnessed the effects of living under a political terror.

What made this so hard to believe was the fact that one associated the Blairs with their cosy little village shop at Wallington and with his parents' quiet home in provincial Southwold. The fact that they had suddenly transplanted themselves to the front line of militant working class resistance against fascism, thereby also exposing themselves to a Communist reign of terror, brought home to one the realities of twentieth-century European politics in a way that all the demonstrations and meetings and Book Clubs and intellectual Marxist poems entirely failed to do.

WHEN THE SECOND WORLD WAR broke out Orwell had already shot his bolt as a front-line combatant. With weak lungs and a Fascist bullet hole in his neck, he had to accept the disappointment of being turned down by Army, Navy and Air Force and resign himself to becoming an energetic sergeant in the Local Defence Volunteers, later known as the Home Guard. I went to the Mediterranean in 1943 and did not see Orwell again until after his wife's death and the publication of *Animal Farm*. His financial situation had improved, but not his health; and I have since heard that both he and Eileen had underfed themselves during the war, in order to share their rations with people whose need they judged to be greater than their own. So in 1946, as a widower with an adopted baby to look after he seemed, in spite of his comparative financial affluence, to be living a more difficult and uncomfortable life than ever; and when he told me he intended in the future to spend the summers in a farmhouse on a Hebridean island I ought to have foreseen that he would contrive to find the most uninhabitable house in the British Isles. His letter inviting me to stay concluded with the ominous words: "It's quite an easy journey really, except that you have to walk the last eight miles."

The house was at the extreme north end of the island of Jura, and about twenty-five miles from its only port and its only shop. The first seventeen miles of road were difficult and the last eight virtually impossible for motor traffic. It was also accessible by sea, if you could control a small boat with an out-board engine in a channel some four miles wide and swept by heavy Atlantic tides. Milk was obtainable from the only neighbor, about two miles away. The next nearest house was eight miles. Orwell and his sister and the baby seemed very happy, and he had ambitious plans for fruit trees and vegetables. For a strong man in perfect health it would have been a good place for a semi-camping holiday; and it had indeed been Orwell's original intention to spend the winters in London. But very soon his health began to make traveling difficult and he stayed there winters as well as summers, except for occasional unavoidable visits to a sanatorium near Glasgow.

As the last eight miles of road were gradually improved it became possible, sometimes, to drive to the nearest village, which was in fact only a big house and some cottages, with no post office and no shop. But the road was never more than a moorland track at best, overgrown with rushes and liable to be washed away in bad weather and, being built on boggy soil, the stones with which the holes were patched soon sank in and had to be replaced. At night the chances were at least even of getting a wheel stuck in one of the boggy open drains which bordered it. After a doctor had told me that Orwell was liable to a hemorrhage if subjected to rough or violent movement I developed a strong reluctance to driving him on this road. "Civilization is Communication" and Orwell had chosen to live in a place where civilization was liable at any moment to collapse. But it was here that he wrote 1984 and during his increasingly rare spells of good health he was certainly happy—working in the garden, fishing for mackerel from a boat, being bullied by his adopted son. He felt that he was at last putting down roots. But in reality it was obvious that he had chosen a too rocky soil.

And that was typical of him. I remember his comment when I told him of an experience of mine in the early 1920's. In those days the Communist Party enjoyed very little prestige in England and was still affiliated to the Labour Party. One day I was at a Labour club in north London and someone said: "You must meet our Communist poet." I was then introduced to a dishevelled-looking man whose name, to my astonishment, I recognized as that of a distinguished member of the Symbolist group. When I told Orwell about this many years later he said: "Ah, but in those days, you see, it *didn't pay* to be a Communist; and it's a pretty safe rule to say about anything that as long as it doesn't pay it's all right." Justice, in other words, is always with the weaker side, and you know which is the weaker side because it does not pay to join it. But he certainly sometimes carried the principle to absurd lengths, and this aspect of him was wittily described by Mr. V. S. Pritchett in an account of how Orwell once advised him that he ought to keep goats. The chief point being, so Mr. Pritchett gathered, that it would put him to a lot of trouble and he would be certain to lose a lot of money; and Orwell got quite carried away with enthusiasm as he expounded the "alluring disadvantages" of the scheme.

In the same way, again, I fear that the near-impossibility of making a tolerably comfortable life there was a positive inducement to Orwell to settle in the remotest corner of the island of Jura.

Anyway, as the months went by, his bad days, when he had to keep to his bed, became more frequent, and finally after three years the day came, in January 1949, when I drove him for the last time over the terrible moorland road on the first stage of the long journey to a sanatorium in Gloucestershire. He had finished 1984 and was very weak, though mentally as active as ever and full of ideas for future work—a novel, and essays on Conrad, Gissing and Evelyn Waugh. In the year of life that remained to him he was to marry again and make plans to go to Switzerland; but he died just before the day fixed for the journey.

One of the last long conversations I had with him was in the train traveling to Gloucestershire, and in the course of it he revealed two quaint pieces of ignorance. From Glasgow the train runs south for about a hundred miles before reaching the English border at Carlisle, but as soon as we were clear of the Glasgow suburbs Orwell remarked: "The weather seems to be just the same in England," and I discovered he thought England began immediately south of Glasgow. At first he couldn't understand my surprise, but he became more interested when I gave the matter a literary slant by pointing out that the part of Scotland whose existence he ignored includes the birthplace of Carlyle, the Burns country, and the Walter Scott country. A little later we were discussing cross-country railway journeys and he wondered if it is possible for the trains of one railway system or company to run on the tracks of another. I told him it was frequently done, but did not investigate this piece of ignorance. Whether he thought the gauges might be different or that the lines of the various railways never joined one another, I do not know. But it seemed odd that he could live in England for nearly fifty years without noticing that its railways, like those of most other countries, not merely use one another's tracks but also frequently use the same stations.

It seems odd, too, that having known one of the most interesting men of his time for a period of twenty years, so many of one's memories should be of trivial conversations like this. But for some reason the memory of them is quaintly endearing.

It is difficult to imagine that anyone who knew Orwell can have any memories of him that are not endearing. One of the chief memories that I retain of this strenuous and self-martyrizing man is the atmosphere of cosiness which he often managed to diffuse. After one of the frequent disastrous expeditions in Jura—returning on foot, for example, at midnight in a misty drizzle having left the truck containing drums of indispensable lamp-oil bogged down somewhere in the hills—one would find that he had come down from his sickroom, stoked up the kitchen fire and made preparations for supper, not merely with efficiency but with a comforting, hospitable, Dickensian glow.

Life on the isle of Jura revealed clearly another not unexpected characteristic, namely, his enthusiasm for heroic and desperate remedies. The district was supposed to be infested by adders and Orwell greatly relished the idea—though I can imagine no one who would be more reluctant to apply it—of the cigar cure for snake bites. This consisted, according to him, in lighting a cigar and then stubbing it out against the wound. I also remember an occasion when his sister dislocated her arm in jumping over a wall. Orwell rushed back to the house and called to me: "You've done first aid, haven't you? Avril's put her arm out. You'll be able to get it back? You just have to jerk it sharply upwards, isn't that it?" The remedy did not work, perhaps because I didn't summon up enough sharpness (Orwell made no attempt to summon up any) and we had to drive the twenty-five miles to the doctor, who was also unsuccessful. So we drove back again and took to the sea, and the arm was finally reset on the mainland, about twelve hours after the accident occurred.

ORWELL was sardonic about the gradual relaxation of wartime restrictions. He professed that he had never believed that the blackout regulations would be withdrawn. Having once got us all neatly blacked out at night with no chinks of light showing, surely "They" would never allow us to show lighted windows again. He said, too, that he had not thrown away his ration book and clothing coupons because the apparent abolition of rationing must be some sort of trap. And when socialists told him that under socialism there would be no such feeling of being at the mercy of unpredictable and irresponsible powers, he commented: "I notice people always say '*under* Socialism.' They look forward to being on top—with all the others underneath, being told what is good for them."

Although entirely without personal malice, he was capable sometimes of surprisingly penetrating personal criticisms; and yet I could never feel that he was at all a reliable judge of character. Or it may be that he kept his shrewdness for what he considered important matters and was simply careless about his own personal interests. At any rate, although he had a lynx eye for humbug and inconsistency in politics and art he seemed often to be unaware when he was being taken advantage of in private life. And he was, or appeared to be, somewhat obtuse about what was going on inside the minds of those nearest to him. But this may have been one of nature's protective devices. For a man with such a gentle heart and so much intelligence and such a tender conscience, life would have been impossible if he had been as sensitive in personal relations as so many cold-hearted egoists are capable of being.

One is tempted to close on that note, but it would be a little too simple. Not that there is anything false in describing Orwell as gentle and unselfish and easygoing in personal relationships. But neither the character he showed in private life nor even the character one may deduce from his books can fully explain his unique quality both as a writer and as a man. Obviously, no full explanation of a man is ever possible. But Orwell did once make a remark to me which seems to give a clue to the obscurer part of his character. Speaking of the first world war, he said that his generation must be marked for ever by the humiliation of not having taken part in it. He had, of course, been too young to take part. But the fact that several million men, some of them not much older than himself, had been through an ordeal which he had not shared was apparently intolerable to him.

This is an example of his exaggerated sense of honor carried to the point of Promethean arrogance. It explains his ruthlessness toward himself and perhaps also his occasional inconsiderateness toward others. And yet it would not be easy to think of many victims of his inconsiderateness, apart from his wife and anyone else who was concerned to counteract his disregard of his own health and safety. But everything in this life has to be paid for and sometimes—although this was not my own experience in the case of Orwell —the price of associating with a man of exceptional disinterestedness and courage is a high one. If the raw material of heroism consists partly of a sort of refined and sublimated egoism, it is to be expected that the progress through life of a man of superior character will leave behind it a more disturbing backwash than the sluggish progress of the average man.

BIBLIOGRAPHICAL NOTE
ON ORWELL'S BOOKS AND ESSAYS

1933   *Down and Out in Paris and London*
1934   *Burmese Days*
1935   *A Clergyman's Daughter*
1936   *Keep the Aspidistra Flying*
1937   *The Road to Wigan Pier*
1938   *Homage to Catalonia*
1939   *Coming up for Air*
1940   *Inside the Whale* (including "Charles Dickens,"
       "Boys' Weeklies" and "Inside the Whale.")
1941   *The Lion and the Unicorn*
1945   *Animal Farm*
1946   *Critical Essays* (American title: *Dickens,
       Dali and Others.* This volume includes "Wells,
       Hitler and the World State," "The Art of
       Donald McGill," "Rudyard Kipling," "W. B.
       Yeats," "Notes on Salvador Dali," "Arthur
       Koestler," "Raffles and Miss Blandish," "In
       Defence of P. G. Wodehouse," and reprints
       of "Charles Dickens" and "Boys' Weeklies.")
1947   *The English People*
1949   *Nineteen-Eighty-Four*
1950   *Shooting an Elephant* (This volume includes
       "Shooting an Elephant," "A Hanging," "How
       the Poor Die," "Lear, Tolstoy and the Fool,"
       "Politics vs. Literature," "Politics and the
       English Language," "Reflections on Gandhi,"
       "The Prevention of Literature," "Second
       Thoughts on James Burnham," and "I Write as

I Please"—the last consisting of selections
from a weekly column in *Tribune*.)

1953   *England, Your England* (The British edition
contains "Why I Write," "Writers and
Leviathan," "Notes on Nationalism,"
"Anti-Semitism in Britain," "Poetry and the
Microphone," "Marrakech," "Looking Back
on the Spanish War," a reprint of "Inside
the Whale," two extracts from *The Road to
Wigan Pier*, and one from *The Lion and the
Unicorn*. The American edition, entitled
Such, Such Were the Joys, contains the
essay of that name but not the two extracts
from *The Road to Wigan Pier*.)

Orwell also contributed to *The Betrayal of the Left*
(1941) and *Victory or Vested Interests?* (1942). He
wrote prefaces for Jack London's *Love of Life* (1946),
Reginald Reynolds' *British Pamphleteers* (1948), and for
the Ukrainian edition of *Animal Farm* (1947). Selections
from his notebooks appeared in *World Review* (June,
1950). Five of his poems were published in *The Adelphi*
between 1933 and 1935. He contributed reviews and
articles to a number of journals, some of which have not
been reprinted, and between 1942 and 1946 made a number of broadcasts.

INDEX